Culture and Customs of the Apache Indians

Apachean Groups—Present Day. (ABC-CLIO)

Culture and Customs of the Apache Indians

VERONICA E. VELARDE TILLER

Culture and Customs of Native Peoples in America

Tom Holm, Series Editor

GREENWOOD

AN IMPRINT OF ABC-CLIO, LLC
Santa Barbara, California • Denver, Colorado • Oxford, England

Library of Congress Cataloging-in-Publication Data

Tiller, Veronica E. Velarde
   Culture and customs of the Apache Indians / Veronica E. Velarde Tiller.
      p. cm. — (Culture and customs of native peoples in America)
   Includes bibliographical references and index.
      ISBN 978–0–313–36452–5 (hard copy : alk. paper) — ISBN 978–0–313–36453–2 (ebook)
   1. Apache Indians. 2. Apache Indians—Social life and customs. I. Title.
   E99.A6T55 2011
   970.004′97—dc22   2010039461

ISBN: 978–0–313–36452–5
EISBN: 978–0–313–36453–2

15 14 13 12 11   1 2 3 4 5

This book is also available on the World Wide Web as an eBook.
Visit www.abc-clio.com for details.

Greenwood
An Imprint of ABC-CLIO, LLC

ABC-CLIO, LLC
130 Cremona Drive, P.O. Box 1911
Santa Barbara, California 93116-1911

This book is printed on acid-free paper ∞

Manufactured in the United States of America

Dedicated to my memory of

Rebecca Monarco Velarde Martinez
[1924–2006]
Great Jicarilla Apache Woman and Mother

Contents

Series Foreword

Since the 1960s, Native and non-Native scholars have diligently sought to disassemble and understand the false and, frankly, harmful stereotypes and images of Native American peoples. Many Americans have recognized that stereotypes of indigenous people are not only often wrong, but have actually fostered adverse political and legal decisions and even sporadic and arbitrary attempts to have whole Native American communities eradicated. The steep and steady decline of the indigenous population, the dissolution of Native governments, and the loss of culture and lands stem from an almost perverse lack of knowledge about Native American peoples.

Despite the dispossession of lands and many, many cultural features, Native American peoples have been astonishingly resilient. White Earth Anishinaabe author Gerald Vizenor, a wordcraftsman of no mean abilities and talents, coined the term "survivance" from the words "survival" and "resistance" to capture the two-fold nature of why indigenous customs and cultures are still alive. The Greenwood Press series *Culture and Customs of Native Peoples in America* attempts not to cast aspersions on the motives, desires, and policies of the Europeans and Euro-Americans who colonized North America, but to highlight, especially to young people and a general audience, the beauty, knowledge, pride, and resiliency of the indigenous peoples of this land. "Survivance" is very real. Native Americans, as our authors show, are not extinct, nor have they become a single, relatively small U.S. ethnic group.

Rather, Native Americans are here today as members of many indigenous nation-states that have utterly unique relationships with the United States. Today, the federal government recognizes 562 American Indian and Native Alaskan tribes and communities that are self-governing and hold certain sovereign rights and powers. Over 1 million people are citizens or members of these nation-states. Nearly 4.5 million people in the United States claim some degree of American Indian or Alaska Native racial heritage.

Most Americans do not quite understand that Native American sovereignty relates specifically to the survival of tribal cultures. When the Europeans came to North American shores, there were hundreds of indigenous peoples, each group with its own territorial boundaries, distinct language, religious customs and ceremonial cycles attuned to the place in which they lived, and a unique and sacred history. All had developed governing bodies that maintained order within and could raise military forces to protect and defend their territories. Each was, therefore, sovereign, but each had different forms of governance, whether by council, kingship, or priesthood. Nearly all of the Native nation-states based their social organization on kinship.

The European colonists came for land and human and natural resources. At first, they attempted to displace the indigenous nation-states or enter into largely unequal and oftentimes destructive trade relationships. Very many Native Americans perished as a result of new, pandemic diseases that were endemic to European populations. Native nations were also caught up in a series of colonial wars that led to further depopulation.

In an effort to end violence and bring about stability, Native nations entered into a series of treaties with foreign powers. When the United States emerged from the stew of colonialism, it continued the treaty-making policies in order to expand its eminent domain from coast to coast. Of course, numerous terrible wars resulted from this policy, but for the most part Native nations and the United States maintained the relationships they created in the treaty-making process. Native nations lost territory and many were displaced from their homelands, but 562 of them have maintained what has been called "limited sovereignty." What this means is that although Native nation-states have certainly lost some of their powers as sovereigns, they have maintained the rights of taxation, territorial integrity, determination of citizenship, and cultural sovereignty. Despite the fact that the U.S. government has violated nearly every one of their treaties with the Native nations, the treaties nevertheless established today's general guarantee that Native peoples can continue as autonomous cultural entities with the ability to change or adapt on their own terms. This is only one of the reasons that Native peoples assert their sovereignty rather than simply become assimilated into the general U.S. society.

Another indigenous people, the Native Hawaiians, were treated similarly. The descendents of Native Hawaiians number over 4 million people. Their own nation-state, established over all the islands by King Kamehameha the Great in 1810, was undermined and finally usurped in 1893. Queen Lili'uokalani was actually imprisoned and replaced by a ruling cabal of businessmen and plantation owners. For a time, these men ruled the islands as "the Republic of Hawaii." In 1898, the United States annexed the islands and the territory eventually became a state of the union in 1959. Since then, Native Hawaiians have adapted their customs and culture to insure their survival. Cultural have multiplied and the Native language has been preserved in place names, ceremonies, and in a number of households.

The *Culture and Customs of Native Peoples in America* series hopes to serve as an exploration of the vibrant cultures and intriguing customs of several North American indigenous groups, from religious practice and folklore to traditional costumes and cuisine. It is an enjoyable and stimulating journey.

Tom Holm
Tucson, Arizona

Preface

THE INVITATION TO participate as a contributor to this series by Greenwood Press was an honor for me. I first saw this as a unique opportunity to help reshape Apache history from historical accounts that were either full of stereotypes or were condescending. I was particularly impressed with the idea of reaching a very wide audience, especially high school students. It is my belief that one's impressions of history, good or bad, are formed when one is in high school. I wrote this account with them in mind. It is a concise guide to Apache cultural, social, and economic history that spans from colonial to modern times. Following the historical Apache trail through time can be daunting, and this account will clarify and elucidate the complex mosaic of Apache life and history into contemporary times.

The focus of this book is on the modern lifestyles of the eight Apache tribes of Arizona, New Mexico, and Oklahoma in all their dimensions, layers, and depth. It will provide an easy way to understand Apache religion without all the mysticism or apologies, but as a legitimate worldview based on a high respect for nature. The artistic expression of the Apache as reflected in art, music, dance, dress, cuisine, will be presented as a link between the past and the present. The social context within which the role of family and tribal identity thrives or is diminished will be presented.

It is almost impossible to provide an account of modern times without the historical context. There are unique circumstances that explain how and why

Apache tribes got to where they are today. Unlike many other Americans, Apache tribes are indigenous to this country, they are a conquered people who assimilated into the dominant society, and they have a special trustee relationship with the U.S. federal government. This account of history explains why they live on Indian reservations, what their modern communities and tribal governments are like and why their economies are in some instances more like Third-World economies, and how, with the commercialization of gaming, they have made unprecedented progress in such a short time.

Lastly, the myriad of issues they face today, like rising crime, a health epidemic, use of dangerous drugs, and a breakdown of the family unit, will be discussed as elements of the realities of life facing modern tribes. A discussion of the core strengths of the Apache character that has brought them through good and bad times will round out the account of the proud people called Apaches.

Acknowledgments

Kaitlin Ciarmiello of Greenwood Press is to be acknowledged for this chance she has given me to make a contribution to the history of my people. I agonized over whether or not this account would be a fair treatment of all the Apache tribes and decided that given the scope, it would be difficult to cover all tribes in all the areas. I consulted with various people from members among my large and ever-growing Jicarilla Apache family, professional colleagues, and respected friends who all have a mutual interest in the presentation of our native history and culture from our perspective. They helped me realize that this book will only be an important beginning in accomplishing my life's dream of writing about my own people. I thank them for their input, comments, and encouragement. Special thanks are extended to Harlan McKosato for his assistance in identifying the critical issues facing Native America at this time in history.

There are always special people to thank when a project of this magnitude and importance is undertaken. My husband David Harrison has supported me throughout the time I was writing, in every way imaginable, and I extend my greatest gratitude to him. My sister Mary Velarde has given me support and encouragement with her faith in me and my work, and I acknowledge her for that. My brother Lindberg Velarde has always willingly shared his knowledge of Apache religion, and no words can express my thanks to him. Roberta Serafin, also my sister, gave me insights and cultural information that made a difference in my writing, and she is to be thanked. My daughters Emmie Frederiks and Christina Harrison have cheered me on the whole way, and they are to be thanked for the power of their encouragement.

Providing me with photographs for consideration were Sheldon Nunez-Velarde, Bob Allen, Tammie Allen, Emmie Frederiks, Bobbienell Vigil, Fred Vigil, Sam Minkler, Lucian Niemeyer, Matthieu Rouge, Tiller Research, Inc., and Dina Kabotie Velarde, and I thank them. Valuable research assistance was given me by Reba June Serafin and Brian Ramirez, especially when I felt like giving up. My gratitude goes out to them. The one person who deserves an extra acknowledgement is my editor and friend, Andrea Hernandez Holm, who without exception is the best editor ever. Most of all, I thank my mother Rebecca Martinez for shaping my life views and perspectives on what it means to be Jicarilla Apache.

Chronology

1000–1500	Apaches migration out of NW Canadian-Alaskan region to Southwest
1492	Christopher Columbus lands in Hispaniola and claims the Americas for Spain
1500s	Apaches settle eastern and southern Arizona, New Mexico, Southeastern Colorado Arizona, western plains regions of Oklahoma and Texas, and northern provinces of Mexico
1511	Spain creates Council of Indies to govern newly discovered lands under laws: *Recopilacion de Leyes de los Reynos de las Indias*
1532	Jesuit theologian Francisco de Vitoria declares Indians are true owners of the conquered lands
1541	Francisco Vásquez de Coronado explores Southwestern U.S.
1541–1600	Apaches acquire the horse
1541–1821	Spanish encounter Apaches
1595	Juan de Oñate begins colonizing the province of New Mexico
1600s	Spanish admit large-scale failure to convert Apaches to Christianity
1700s	Spanish give name of Jicarilla (basket makers) to one band

1765–1780	Hostilities between Spanish and Apaches intensify
1786	Viceroy of New Spain, Bernardo de Gálvez implements a new policy of settling the Apaches in villages near presidios
1789	U.S. Constitution states that only Congress can conduct trade with Indian tribes and creates special relationship with Indian tribes
1821	Mexico gains its independence from Spain
1848	Treaty of Guadalupe Hidalgo signed between Mexico and U.S.
1851 & 1855	Jicarilla Apache sign treaties with U.S., but they are not ratified by Congress
1852	Mescalero Apache sign treaty with the United States on July 1
1853	Gadsden Purchase
1866	Colony of Virginia sets one-quarter blood quantum requirements to determine Indian heritage
1870	Fort Apache Army Post built at White Mountain on May 16
1871	Camp Grant Massacre
	Camp Verde Reservation and White Mountain-San Carlos Reservation created by Executive Order of November 9
1872	Camp Verde Reservation and White Mountain-San Carlos
	Reservation created by Executive Order of December 14
1874	U.S. removal policy designates concentration of all Western Apaches on San Carlos Apache Reservation
1875	Camp Verde Reservation is abolished and the Yavapais and Apaches are sent to San Carlos
1876	Ojo Caliente Reservation abolished
1879	Captain Richard Henry Pratt inaugurates the federal educational program by establishing the Indian Industrial School at Carlisle, Pennsylvania, which becomes model for all Indian schools
1880–1884	Guerilla warfare between Apache and U.S. Army
1880	General Crook increases his troops
1884	First Indian boarding school established at Mescalero
	Albuquerque Indian School established
1886	General Nelson A. Miles replaces General Crook

1886–1913	Chiricahua Apaches are prisoners of war
1886	Geronimo surrenders to General Nelson Miles at Skeleton Canyon, Arizona Territory on September 4
	Beginning of Assimilationist Era
1887	On February 11 permanent reservation was established by executive order for the Jicarilla Apache Tribe of New Mexico
	General Allotment Act of 1887 (Dawes Act) passed by Congress
	Government mandates that all instruction at Indian schools be in English
1890	Santa Fe and Phoenix Indian Schools established
1892	Congress authorizes the Commissioner of Indian Affairs to make school attendance compulsory on Indian reservations
1894	Chiricahua Apaches resettled at Fort Sill, Oklahoma
1897	White Mountain-San Carlos Reservation was separated into two reservations on June 17 by an Act of Congress
1903	Indian Boarding School established on Jicarilla Apache Reservation
1913	Portion of Fort Sill Chiricahua Apaches move to Mescalero Apache Reservation in New Mexico
1914	World-renowned Apache sculptor Allan Houser is born on June 30
1920s	Livestock industry established on Apache reservations
1928	Merriam Report
1934	Indian Reorganization Act passed by Congress on June 4
1937–1938	Arizona and New Mexico Apache tribes adopt IRA constitutions and bylaws and establish tribal governments
1937	Johnson-O'Malley Act provides public education for Indian students
1952	Jicarilla Apache Tribe creates Chester E. Faris Scholarship fund for higher education
1960	War on Poverty program begins under Johnson administration
1961	Ski Apache opens on the Mescalero Apache Reservation
1965	Elementary and Secondary Education Act was passed to meet the special educational needs of low-income families

1972	Indian Education Act encourages parental involvement in education of Indian children; establishes U.S. Office of Indian Education
	Tonto Apaches of Payson, Arizona, receive federal recognition as Indian tribe
1974	Tonto Apache Tribe receives 85-acre reservation
1976	Fort Sill Apache Tribe ratifies constitution and bylaws on October 30
1977	Jicarilla Apache Tribe becomes first tribe to own and operate its own oil and gas production company
1978	U.S. Congress passes the Indian Freedom of Religion Act, which guarantees the Native Americans the constitutional right to freedom of religion
1982	*Mescalero Apache Tribe v. State of New Mexico* recognizes tribal authority over management of fish and wildlife resources on reservations
1988	National Indian Gaming Regulatory Act passed to allow gaming on Indian reservations
1992	Yavapai Apache Tribe changes name to Yavapai-Apache Nation
1995	San Carlos Apache Tribe opens its cultural center in Peridot
1996	The Native American Housing Assistance and Self-Determination Act (NAHASDA) signed into law on October 26
1999	Jicarilla Apache Tribe honored by Harvard University's Honoring Nations program for its Wildlife and Fisheries program
2000	White Mountain Apache Tribe honored by Harvard University's Honoring Nations program for its Wildlife and Recreation program
	San Carlos Apache Tribe honored by Harvard University's Honoring Nations program for its Elders Advisory Council
	Fort Apache and San Carlos reservations are ranked in top 25 most populous Indian reservations in the United States
	Population: 161,755 Apaches counted in 2000 U.S. Census
2006	Esther Martinez Act passed by U.S. Congress. This act provides a competitive grant program to promote, expand, replicate, or build on successful innovative language programs through projects like survival schools, teacher training, and immersion language restoration programs

1

Introduction to the Apache Tribes

WHO ARE THE APACHES?

The historical identification of the Apache people—who they are, where they came from, and how they got to where they are—is at best complex, perplexing, and difficult, even for people who consider themselves Apache scholars. There are several reasons for this mosaic of complexity. Since the first contact between the Apaches and the Spanish in the Southwest in the sixteenth century, the Spanish chroniclers, missionaries, the military, and government officials could not keep track of the Apaches, much less identify them by name. As nomadic peoples they moved from place to place over their huge territories. When the Spanish thought they had identified an Apache band with a particular physical location, like a mountain or river, and assigned them a name, the following year either the band moved on or another band took their place. Apaches were indeed true nomads. The Spanish accounts are replete with names for Apache bands that did not survive over time.

The Americans inherited this situation as they encountered the Apache people beginning in the early 1800s. It was not until the *Apache Wars* and when they were settled onto reservations that the Apache people were finally identified by tribal groups and affiliations. As the U.S. military forces fought the Apaches, they began to recognize bands and their leading warriors as belonging to a larger tribe or a particular location, like the Chiricahua who inhabited southwestern New Mexico and southeastern Arizona. During the Indian wars, some of the smaller Apache bands were consolidated with either larger bands or groups of bands from a certain area. For example, the White Mountain Apaches of east-central Arizona consist of historic Apache bands such as the Coyoteros, Arivaipas, Cibecue, and Mogollons.[1] The San Carlos Indian Reservation of southeastern Arizona has Apache bands that were historically known as Gila Apaches, Mimbreños, and others.

The majority of Apache bands were placed on their own reservations by the 1870s, but there were Arizona Apache bands who ended up with other tribes, like those related to the Yavapai, Mohave, or Yuman tribes. The people at the Camp Verde Reservation located in north-central Arizona are also known as Yavapai-Apaches. These Yavapai-Apaches were taken to the San Carlos Indian Reservation in 1871 but were finally allowed to return to the Payson and Verde Valley areas in the 1890s. It was not until 1972 that the Tonto Apache Tribe of Payson, Arizona, obtained recognition from the federal government as an official Indian tribe, and in 1974 they received their 85-acre reservation.[2]

The Apache tribes of Oklahoma have a long and complex history that involves early consolidation or merging with other Plains tribes. For example, the Kiowa-Apaches today identify themselves more as Kiowa than Apache. This group of Apaches will not be considered in this textbook. The small band known as the Apache Tribe of Oklahoma remains, in large part, a mystery due to a lack of written materials about them, but because they do exist as a tribe today they will be dealt with in this text. The Fort Sill Apache Tribe of Oklahoma are the remnants of the Chiricahua Apaches of Arizona, who were prisoners of war in the period of 1886–1913, first in Florida, then Alabama, and finally resettled in Oklahoma. A small group of Lipan Apaches, whose aboriginal territory included the Plains region of New Mexico, Texas, and the northern Mexican provinces, are found on the Mescalero Apache Indian Reservation. They were moved there in 1903. Because they are nearly extinct as a people known and identified as Lipan Apache, their history will not be explored in this book, but their survival will be acknowledged through their presence on the Mescalero Apache Reservation.

During the late 1800s, scholars (mainly anthropologists and linguists) began studying the culture of the Apache people. As a result, the Apache people were divided into and classified as Western and Eastern Apaches. The Eastern Apaches consisted of the Apaches who hunted the buffalo in the plains of Texas and the northeastern portions of New Mexico and western Oklahoma, like the Lipan and Kiowa-Apaches. Today the only Eastern Apache group is the Jicarilla Apache of northern New Mexico. The Western Apaches are those in Arizona, the Mescalero Apaches of New Mexico, and the Fort Sill Apaches of Oklahoma.

The better-known Apache tribes are the Western Apaches of Arizona, particularly the Chiricahuas, due to U.S. attention to this band. Beginning in the late nineteenth century, the Chiricahua have been present in national newspapers and media coverage. The Apache Wars received a great deal of coverage, and warriors such as Cochise, Victorio, and Geronimo have become notorious in popular U.S. culture. Popular stereotypes of the Apaches emerged as early as the late 1800s and the Apaches continue to fascinate audiences, evident by their perpetuation in U.S. and foreign literature and film.

Today in Arizona, New Mexico, and Oklahoma, there are eight Apache tribes. Three of the tribes, the White Mountain Apache Tribe, the San Carlos Apache Tribe, and the Tonto Apache Tribe, are located on their own reservations. The name of the reservation on which the White Mountain Apache live is the Fort Apache Indian Reservation. The other Arizona tribe with a sizeable Apache population is the Camp Verde Yavapai-Apache Nation. The Jicarilla Apache Nation and Mescalero Apache Tribe are located in north-central and southeastern New Mexico respectively. Two small Apache tribes are located at Apache and Fort Sill, Oklahoma.

Young girl at Goijiya on Jicarilla Reservation. (Photo by Emmie Frederiks)

In contemporary times, Apache people identify themselves by the tribes that they belong to if they are officially enrolled in that tribe; if they are not enrolled members they identify themselves by the tribe that they are descended from. Membership in an Indian tribe is usually defined by tribal constitutions and based on Indian blood quantum, which means that an Indian person has to have a certain amount of Indian blood to be eligible for tribal membership. This blood quantum requirement was instituted by the federal government during 1930s when Apache tribes' constitutions were approved. There are a few of the tribes throughout the United States that have a high Apache blood quantum requirement for membership. The Jicarilla Apache, for example, has a 3/8 blood quantum requirement despite their low tribal enrollment figures.

The U.S. Census for 2000 provides the most accurate data on the number of Apache people located on the various Apache Indian reservations, although the goal of the Census is to count all people in a given geographical area, not to determine their exact tribal or ethnic identities. For example, according the 2000 Census, there were 12,429 people on the Fort Apache Indian Reservation, but the tribal enrollment in 2004 listed 13,556 members for that tribe.[3] The discrepancy may be accounted for because large numbers of Apaches from all tribes live off reservations in small towns and in urban areas throughout the United States.

Culturally, all the Apache people and Apache tribes are Southern Athapaskans, sharing a common language, religion, and social customs. They are divided into Eastern and Western Apaches because of their cultural differences, which can be connected to their physical environment, their particular "brand" of religious practices, and the cultural influences from Indian tribes and non-Indian neighbors throughout their history. Historically, they share a common history of the invasion of their lands by the Spanish and later, the Americans. In resisting invasion, they have gone to war to protect their lands and preserve their way of life; they have been militarily defeated, confined to Indian reservations, and subjected to the policies of the federal government, which required their assimilation into U.S. society. They have shared the experience of seeing their culture ridiculed, and their religion nearly wiped out, being separated from their children who were taken to residential boarding schools, and suffering from the historical trauma of these experiences.

The Apache people have survived the historic experiences and have rebuilt their homes, established modern tribal governments and economies, and have made progress in all areas of their lives. The Apache people have been lucky in that they have had the

U.S. government establish large reservations in or near their original homelands. The Fort Apache Reservation, the San Carlos Apache Reservation, and the Mescalero Apache Reservation are located on aboriginal Apache territories, and these three reservations together consist of just under 4 million acres. On these lands and on other Apache reservations, the Apaches basically remained isolated for a number of years and were able to keep much of their culture and religion intact despite the official onslaught to do away with their traditional culture and religion. The exception to this settlement pattern has been the Chiricahua Apaches, who were prisoners of war in 1886–1913 and finally resettled at Fort Sill, Oklahoma, in 1894; a portion of them chose to join their brethren on the Mescalero Apache Reservation in 1913.[4]

The Apache tribes are, historically and in modern times, similar and different from each other in their lifestyles, economies, governments, and in the issues they face. Because of their cultural similarities, they were treated in the same manner by the peoples invading their homelands, from the Spanish and Mexicans during colonial times, to the American people and the U.S. government. The relationship between the United States and the Apache tribes was governed by federal Indian policies that were heavily influenced by historic events occurring throughout the United States. The federal Indian policies largely determined the "fate" of the Indian tribes. While many of the policies were intended to assimilate, isolate, and even eradicate Indian people, many tribes, such as the Apaches, have survived and have much to show for their endurance. What the Apaches share and have in common today are the large reservation land bases blessed with an abundance of natural resources and scenic landscapes. The Apache people also share a reverence for their lands.

Because they have reservation environments with similar natural resources, the Apaches have tribal governments and economies that reflect their concern for the proper use and protection of those environments. In the arena of social and health concerns, they all face issues like offering educational opportunities to all members of the tribe, making housing and jobs available to members, and preserving their culture, as well as dealing with issues like diabetes, alcoholism, high educational dropout rates, lack of adequate law enforcement, and the ever-persistent issues of poverty and unemployment.

Today, although the Apache tribes are separated by great physical distances, they maintain their base Athapaskan cultural similarities, especially in their religion and worldviews, language, and social customs.

ANTHROPOLOGICAL INFORMATION ABOUT ATHAPASKAN MIGRATION INTO THE SOUTHWEST

According to anthropologists (scientists who study man, his origins, social habits, development, customs, and culture), the Apaches migrated out of the northwestern Canadian-Alaskan region between about 1000 and 1500. However, the Apaches have their own beliefs about their origins (this subject will be covered in chapter on religion). Many scholars believe that the ancestors of Apaches migrated first into the Western Plains in the current states of Kansas and Nebraska, and by the 1500s into New Mexico, Arizona, Texas, and northern Mexico. By the 1500s the Apaches had settled in territories that are now eastern and southern Arizona, much of New Mexico, southeastern Colorado, western Oklahoma, the panhandles of Oklahoma and Texas, west-central and southern Texas, and the border areas of the northern provinces of Mexico.[5]

The Apache Athapaskan culture changed under the influence of the Pueblo people who lived in the Rio Grande River Valley in New Mexico and the Plains Indians who lived in the current states of Texas, Colorado, and Oklahoma. The people also adapted to their particular physical environments that defined their lifestyles. The Apache bands lived over a wide area that consisted of mountains, valleys, plateaus, and plains. The culture, especially of the Eastern Apaches, was influenced by the buffalo found on the Plains, the use of the tepee from the Plains Indians, and the horse that was introduced by the Spanish. The Spanish also influenced the material culture through trade for items like guns, cloth, blankets, and alcohol. The Apaches have borrowed many Spanish words for items that were not native to their culture. Over the years these cultural influences blended into characteristics that define the Apache people.

The people call themselves *Diné* or *Indé*, meaning "the people," but others call them Apache. The origin of the name comes from *apachu*, meaning "enemy" in the Zuni Pueblo language. The Navajo people are classified as one of the seven Southern Athapaskan—or Apachean-speaking—groups of the U.S. Southwest. The other six Southern Athapaskan groups are the Chiricahua, Jicarilla, Kiowa-Apache, Lipan, Mescalero, and Western Apache. Linguistically, the Southern Athapaskans are divided into two groups. The eastern group includes the Jicarilla, Lipan, and Kiowa-Apache. The Mescalero Apache are often classified with the eastern Apaches. The western group has two major language subdivisions, the Navajo and the Western Apache. The Western Apache language group consists of the San Carlos, White River, Cibecue, and the Southern and Northern Tonto dialects.[6] The Navajo will be excluded in this study.

TRADITIONAL APACHE LANDS AND PHYSICAL ENVIRONMENT

Jicarilla Apache traditional homelands were located in northeastern New Mexico, southern Colorado, and the panhandles of Texas and Oklahoma. The Lipan occupied central and southern Texas and areas of northern

Mexico. The Mescalero and Chiricahua Apaches called southwestern New Mexico, southeastern Arizona, and adjoining areas of the Mexican province of Chihuahua their homelands. The Mescalero lived east of the Pecos River in New Mexico and on into northwestern Texas. The Western Apache lands covered large portions of the central-eastern Arizona area.

The Apaches considered their homelands sacred. Each tribe has identified certain mountain peaks and ranges that are roughly located in the four cardinal directions (east, south, west, and north) as definitions of their sacred boundaries. Although some of the Eastern and Western Apache bands farmed, like all other Apaches, their main subsistence activities consisted of hunting and gathering. The Eastern Apaches hunted the buffalo on the Plains, which brought them into contact with various Plains tribes. The Eastern Apaches adopted the horse, the material culture, and the practice of warfare and raiding from the Plains Indians. Due to the abundance of wildlife, the Jicarillas hunted primarily large animals. The mountain sheep were hunted in the southern Rocky Mountains, antelopes in the eastern flatlands of New Mexico, and deer and elk throughout the mountains and foothills. Smaller animals like beaver, rabbit, squirrels, and prairie dogs were also hunted, but on a limited basis.

Generally, the Apaches, like all other Native Americans, held wildlife and plant life sacred and deserving of respect and veneration. Animals that are considered spiritually significant because of their role in the religion and worldview of the Apaches, past and present, are various species of eagle, deer, bear, mountain lion, coyote, and buffalo. All plants and animals are important to the balance of the natural environment and the ecosystems. Hunting was never done just for the sake of killing animals. All parts of the animals were put to use for a good purpose. The animals provided not only food, but materials that were used for shelter, clothing, tools, and religious ceremonial objects. Hides from the large animals were used for tepee covers, robes and blankets, bags, sinew for thread, rawhide for ropes, ties, straps, and tanned skins for clothing, moccasins, and a host of household items. Birds and animals like eagles, mountain lions, wildcats, and land turtles were taken for their feathers, furs, and other body parts for clothing and religious objects.

In addition to hunting, the Apaches gathered a wide variety of wild berries and wild fruits, acorns, mescal, piñon and pine nuts, and nondomesticated natural foods like parsley, onions, spinach, and edible grasses, including those that grow in swampy areas in and around bodies of water. A large assortment of herbs, tubers, bark, tree gum, leaves, and grasses from the mountains, valleys, and plains areas were gathered at different seasons of the year for medicinal purposes. As master basket weavers, the Apache women collected an array of willows, branches, and berries for color dyes at various locations throughout their homelands. Jicarilla potters obtained micaceous clay for pottery from special areas throughout the mountains of northern New Mexico.

Perhaps what best characterizes the Apache tribes is their religion, as defined by their beliefs and practices, their language, and their philosophies. It is the common religion that unifies the various Apache tribes. Their religion consists of a set of fundamental beliefs that man is a part of the natural world and that all living things, whether plants or animals, are critically important to the balance of nature.[7] The source of all religious thought, beliefs, and ideas are the Creation stories, but each of the Apache tribes have their own versions and interpretations that are localized and customized to their own sacred lands. The religion of the Apache requires that all of nature's creatures, plant life, and all natural forms of energy like the sun, the wind, and lightning, and resources like bodies of water, are to be respected. Apache religious ceremonies are conducted to cure people of various illnesses, to give thanks to nature for its bounties and gifts, and to ask the Great Spirit for things such as courage, a good harvest, healthy children, and love and understanding among all peoples.[8] Most of all, the Apaches conduct the ceremonies to keep the balance in nature and in the universe. These ceremonies are required by the Apache religion. Many of the traditional ceremonies still take place today among the Apache people. The Apache tribes share in common the Girl's Puberty Ceremony but it, like other shared customs, is carried out in different ways. The Western Apache Tribes also have in common the *Gah* or Mountain Spirit dances and ceremonies. Only the Jicarilla Apache have the Bear Dance and the ceremonial relay races.

THE SPANISH ENCOUNTER THE APACHES: 1541 TO 1821

After they arrived in Mesoamerica and began to colonize the lands there, the Spanish moved northward into what are now California, Arizona, New Mexico, and Texas, becoming the first Europeans to have contact with the people of the American Southwest. Spanish military forces were accompanied by representatives of the Catholic Church, first the Franciscans and later the Jesuits. The colonization process in the Southwest went hand in hand with the mission movement. While the Church attempted to convert all Indians to Catholicism, the military worked to remove them from the lands. The process involved the establishment of a mission on a land base, usually near a military fort, and often near an established Indian community. The conversion of the Indians was more easily achieved with everyone living so closely together. Because the Apaches in Arizona, New Mexico, and Texas in particular were nomadic, it proved challenging to the Church to maintain contact with them, and attempts to convert them were largely unsuccessful.

From 1541 through the 1700s, the Spanish colonizers concentrated their efforts in establishing relations with the Apaches of northeastern New Mexico and the plains of northern Texas. The ancestors of the Jicarilla Apaches were first encountered by Spaniards in 1541, when Francisco Vásquez de Coronado and his soldiers were exploring the area of what is now northeastern New Mexico and the immediate plains to the east. The Spaniards called the Apaches they met between the Canadian and Red Rivers *Querechos*. These Apaches were on the plains hunting buffalo.

In 1595, Juan de Oñate began colonizing the province of New Mexico. While the Spaniards concentrated their missionary efforts among the Pueblos of the Rio Grande Valley, they also tried to convert the Apaches in this area to the Catholic religion. Throughout the 1600s the Spanish by and large left the Apaches alone, having failed to convert them to Christianity. The Spanish noticed a distinction among the Apaches living in northeastern New Mexico. One Apache group had adopted a semisedentary lifestyle of living on rancherias that featured horticulture, along with irrigation and pottery making. It was not until the early 1700s that the Spanish called this band of Apaches the Jicarilla Apaches. Jicarilla means "basket maker" in the Spanish language.

The situation in Arizona, southern New Mexico, and the Spanish borderlands along the northern provinces of Chihuahua, Sonora, and Nueva Viscaya was radically different from the situation in the northern areas. The Spanish colonizers assumed the right to settle on lands of their choosing—of course they chose those areas that offered access to natural resources. These areas were often the same ones that the Apache tribes had been using for centuries. The Apaches resisted the Spanish presence with force. It was in these regions in particular that Apaches practiced raiding. The introduction of the horse provided the Apaches with the ability to quickly ride in and out of the settlements and travel long distances before they were discovered. It has been suggested that the Apaches raided not to drive the Spanish out, but to exploit the convenient and new economic resources, like agricultural products and livestock, because they did not engage in "mass killing and the wide-scale destruction of enemy property."[9]

New Spain responded to the threats against Spanish settlements by establishing military presidios in its far northern regions (now the Southwestern U.S. and northern Mexico) and engaging in military skirmishes with the Apaches. Between 1765 and 1780, the hostilities between the Apaches and Spanish intensified, forcing the Spanish to admit that their plans to exterminate the Apaches were unrealistic and unattainable. In 1786 the viceroy of New Spain, Bernardo de Gálvez, implemented a new policy of settling the Apaches in villages near presidios, where they would be supplied with food, clothing, inferior firearms, and alcoholic drinks. The intent of this policy was to create dependence, promote social disorganization, and to subdue their will to fight. Until about 1825, this Spanish policy of settling the Apaches worked, as evidenced by the decrease in raiding and the expansion of Spanish ranches and mining communities into southern Arizona.[10]

THE MEXICAN PERIOD: RELATIONS WITH THE APACHE

When Mexico gained its independence from Spain in 1821 in the Mexican War of Independence, the new Mexican government was unable or unwilling to uphold many of Spain's policies. Beset with serious financial problems, Mexico could no longer subsidize the Apaches, and they left the presidios to regroup in their traditional territories. By 1831, the Western Apaches had resumed their intensive raiding activities along the northern Mexican frontier provinces. Apache raiding into these areas became commonplace.

THE U.S. PERIOD: THE SIGNING OF TREATIES AND ESTABLISHMENT OF RESERVATIONS

In 1848, with the signing of the Treaty of Guadalupe Hidalgo by which the Southwest became a part of the United States, Mexicans were guaranteed that the Indians would be prevented from raiding across the border. However, Congress ignored the problem and left Mexico and the U.S. settlers to fend for themselves as the Apache raiding increased. The United States did not change its attitude until the Gadsden Purchase of 1853, when it made cursory efforts to sign treaties with the various Apache bands both in New Mexico and Arizona. In New Mexico, the Mescalero entered into a treaty with the United States that created their reservation on July 1, 1852. Hostilities with the Mescaleros continued until 1862 when General James H. Carleton instigated sustained military action against them and confined them to the Fort Sumner Reservation, from which they later escaped. Later, through executive orders during the 1870s and 1880s, their reservation was enlarged. The Jicarilla Apaches also signed treaties in 1851 and 1855 that were to have created a reservation for them, but the treaties were not ratified. It was not until February 11, 1887, that a permanent reservation was established by executive order for the Jicarilla Apaches.

The United States established several military posts throughout Apache country to lure the Apaches to settle close by. Through Indian agencies (the administrative arm of the Department of the Interior), food rations and annuities were sporadically handed out to prevent starvation among the Apaches, often enough for the Apaches to become dependent on them. In the meantime, Anglo settlers and prospectors began to intrude upon the domain of the Western Apaches. At first, the people were wary but peaceful, but when it became clear that the new settlers sought to control the Apaches and usurp their territory, the people responded with open hostility. This resulted in a dramatic 40-year war of epic proportions, ending with the irreversible defeat of the Western Apaches and their permanent relocation to reservations.

In the decade of the 1870s the Camp Verde Reservation and a joint White Mountain-San Carlos Reservation were created by two executive orders of November 9, 1871, and December 14, 1872.[11] By this time Congress had abolished the practice of entering into treaties with Indian tribes. The White Mountain-San Carlos Reservation was separated into two reservations on June 17, 1897 by an act of Congress.[12] The Camp Verde Reservation was abolished in 1875 when the Yavapais and Apaches were sent to San Carlos.[13]

On May 16, 1870, an Army post known as Fort Apache was built on the White Mountain Apache portion of the reservation. President Grant placed General George S. Crook in charge of the Arizona Territory. Following the Camp Grant Massacre in 1871, during which a combined mob of enraged citizens from Tucson and Papago Indians (Tohono O'odham), slaughtered more than 75 Western Apache women and children, the federal government implemented a new "peace policy" in Arizona, calling for the collection of all Apaches on reservations by military force. To enforce the orders, U.S. army soldiers killed a large band of innocent Yavapais in an incident that became known as Massacre at Skeleton Canyon. The civilian authorities were no less culpable: many of the problems on the reservation have been attributed to their administrative mismanagement, especially in overseeing the relocation of Apaches.[14] The most hostile toward relocation were those Chiricahua bands under Cochise and later Victorio, who were assigned in 1870 to the newly established Ojo Caliente Reservation in western New Mexico.

THE U.S. REMOVAL POLICIES AND THE APACHE WARS

In 1874 the Department of the Interior reenergized its removal policy designed to concentrate all the Western Apaches on the San Carlos Apache Reservation. In 1876 the Ojo Caliente Reservation was abolished. This action created a chain reaction of hostilities that both sides forever regretted. For the next decade the Chiricahua Apaches were at war with the U.S. military forces. Victorio's band absolutely refused to go to the San Carlos Reservation, and for several years he and his supporters created nothing but havoc with their raiding across the border and causing terror to the inhabitants of New Mexico.[15]

In 1880, a thousand U.S. troops arrived to augment General Crook's Apache scouts and the Mexican troops. Geronimo and his Chiricahua band were off and on the San Carlos Reservation from 1880 to 1884 waging guerilla warfare against the U.S. Army. General Crook managed to corral Geronimo in 1884. It was thought that peace was restored when Geronimo and his band settled near Fort Apache. This was only an illusion, as Geronimo and his Apaches again took to the mountain haunts and renewed the military conflict.

In 1886 General Nelson A. Miles replaced Crook and was eventually credited with bringing the Apache Wars to an end. Miles's strategy was to replace the Apache scouts with Army regulars, but he still had to rely on them to assist his subordinates in negotiating Geronimo's surrender on September 4, 1886. Under the terms of surrender Geronimo and the entire Chiricahua Tribe, innocent or not, were exiled as prisoners of war to Fort Marion and Fort Pickens, Florida. The ultimate insult to the Apache people was how Miles exiled his Apache scouts, although they were officially enlisted members of the Army and had faithfully served the enemies of their people. The Chiricahuas were later taken to Mt. Vernon, Alabama, then to Fort Sill, Oklahoma, in 1894 after an arduous campaign by various organizations that were outraged by Miles's actions.[16] In 1913 the Chiricahuas were given the opportunity to resettle on the Mescalero Apache Reservation in New Mexico. Some chose to go to New Mexico, but by 1913 Fort Sill was already home to a large number of Chiricahua.

THE ASSIMILATIONIST ERA

With the end of the Apache Wars, all Apache tribes were settled onto their respective reservations. The era from the 1880s to 1934 is the period during which American Indians began to be viewed as the "vanishing race." It was expected that they would be extinct by the next century. It was the view of the government and Christian sects that the Indians had no choice but to become assimilated into U.S. society. The U.S. government began "civilizing" the Indians through various measures, like mandating that all Indian children attend residential boarding schools where they were to abandon their cultural ways. If they did not comply they were severely punished. Parents of recalcitrant students found themselves either in jail or denied their government rations.

On the reservation, the Apaches were expected to become yeoman farmers in the image of the Midwestern farmer. Yet the Apaches were located on the lands that were least arable, with no water resources available for irrigation or the practical knowledge of how to farm. The best lands and water had been taken by U.S. settlers.

It was the policy of the government that the religion of Indians was to be squashed and forever eliminated. Measures of all kinds were taken to end religious ceremonies and practices. Indians were to eventually become part of

U.S. life, yet they were denied their basic right of freedom of religion. Every psychological strategy to cause trauma, distress, lack of self-confidence, depression, and self-denial was used against the Apaches to attain the goal of "civilization." Perhaps worst of all was that they were expected to be thankful for the attention and good graces they received from their oppressors.

It was during this era of assimilation that the Apaches lost many cultural ways, yet because of their isolated locations, they also managed to keep much of their culture compared to other Indian tribes throughout the United States. The forced assimilation did cause them to abide by the "rules" and eventually many of them became successful ranchers and livestock owners. Large numbers of children learned to read and write the English language. Inroads were also made by the Christian churches that were located on the reservations. Many Apache people gave up their religion and accepted Christianity.

Today, despite the physical distance separating them, the similarities among the Athapaskan Apache tribes are apparent in their cultural arts, music, and dance. Their modern lifestyles are characterized by the rural location of their reservation communities. In large part, their relationship with the federal government as ward-trustee has defined their quality and type of housing, their educational opportunities and levels of educational attainment, and the amount of employment available on their reservations.

LANGUAGE, ART, MUSIC, DANCE, AND TRADITIONAL DRESS

It is the language that links the Apache tribes to each other, and it is what makes them one cultural family. Fundamentally, they share in common a religion and a language. Of the eight Apache tribes, only the Jicarilla Apache speak an eastern dialect of the language. The other seven speak the western dialect of the Apachean language. The Apache people who are fluent in the language are those that are 50 years old or older. The overall rate of language fluency ranges from a high of 50 percent among the San Carlos Apaches to an average of about 30 percent among the White Mountain Apaches, Mescalero Apaches, and the Jicarilla Apaches. There are no fluent speakers among the Oklahoma Apache Tribes.

All the tribes have made concerted efforts in the last several decades to preserve, maintain, and revive their native languages, with limited success. The historical suppression of the Apache language as mandated by federal Indian policies has been a major factor in the decline of the use of the language today. The Apache societies did not have a written language until the late 1970s. In creating a written language they have adapted the English alphabet using diacritical marks and symbols to represent the different sounds used in the Apache language. Establishing a written language has been marred not only with the reputation created by those responsible for its suppression but the fact that the language is culture-based. Without the culture, the language, within the context of modern society, often does not make sense. In addition, the Apache traditional religion, philosophy, history, stories, songs, and social customs are based on the oral tradition. Creating a written system has not been easy. Not only is the language structure difficult because it has a rich word formation with a great deal of synthesis and a high degree of fusion, but one word can have multiple meanings. The meanings are culturally based and cannot easily be translated into the English language. Nonetheless, the Apache tribes are determined to use written methods in preserving their languages. Offering language classes at schools and cultural centers has been the major approach to facilitate fluency by the tribes. Circumstances like available teachers and adequate funding have curbed the success rate, but building on their past failures and successes, the Apache tribes are committed to reviving and maintaining their languages.

As with their languages, there has been a surge and growth in the promotion of Apache cultural arts, like painting, basket making, and pottery. With a renewed sense of pride and identity, the preservation of Apache culture has reached new heights both by individuals and the tribe. Many individuals have become internationally and nationally well known in the arts, which have their foundation in their heritage but are based in modern times. Tribes have combined cultural events and activities with their affinity for the natural environment to create a tourism and recreation industry. A cultural renaissance has occurred, with an increase in the participation of Apache people in tribal ceremonies like the puberty feasts, mountain spirit ceremonies, and related social events. The visibility of the Apache traditional dress at ceremonies, social events, and official tribal events both on and off the reservations is testimony to a return of Apache ways in modern times. The contemporary culture links the past with the present. Despite the historical setbacks, the Apache tribal arts and culture have entered a new phase of renewal and revival.

MODERN LIFESTYLE, HOUSING, EDUCATION, AND EMPLOYMENT

The modern Apache lifestyle is directly related to the rural location of their reservations in the U.S. Southwest. Their past and recent progress in the improvement or lack of improvement of housing conditions, the educational achievement and its failures, and the employment situation are defined by their historical and legal relationship with the U.S. federal government. Through the changes in federal Indian policies in recent decades and the commercialization of Indian gaming, Apache people finally have a lifestyle of modernity, with decent housing, community facilities including hospitals, schools, cultural centers, and recreation facilities, an increase in employment, and educational opportunities. Despite the recent progress, the challenges of inadequate housing, high unemployment, and low educational achievement levels still face the tribes.

SOCIAL CUSTOMS, MARRIAGE, GENDER, CHILDREN, AND CUISINE

The persistence of Apache culture from ancient times to modern times is a theme that still governs social customs, the family, gender roles, and even the food that is eaten. The agent of social change for the Apaches has been the dominant society. Apache people have selected and adopted most elements of general U.S. society since the late nineteenth century when they were placed on their reservations. They willingly accepted some changes and rejected others. In many cases, they were forced to accept the ways of U.S. society, but even those that they accepted were modified to meet their needs, likes, and dislikes. Apache families in many ways are more similar to U.S. nuclear families, influenced by the national economy, the educational systems, the media, and popular culture. In short, they have a homogenized or mixed society consisting of Apache and U.S. ways.

MODERN APACHE GOVERNMENTS AND ECONOMIES

The Indian Reorganization Act of 1934 (IRA) helped to reverse the trend of forced assimilation. The IRA stopped the allotment of Indian lands, allowed for Indian tribes to establish tribal governments, provided assistance with loans for economic development, and ended education practices that attempted to wipe out tribal cultures. With this new law the Apaches moved into the modern times and, in many ways, on their own terms.

Prior to the white settlements of Arizona and New Mexico, the Apache tribes had millions of acres of land to hunt and gather. When the white men arrived, they took the best farmlands, watered areas, green fertile valleys, and left the desert lands and mountainous country to the Apaches. This caused a lot of conflict and eventually war. During the days of the Indian agencies, the Apaches confined to reservations were issued rations of food, clothing, and small amounts of farming tools to begin farming the barren lands. Much of the rations had been promised in the treaties and agreements. The government policy of assimilation dictated that the Apache Indians become farmers. Unlike most Americans, they did not have the choice of becoming anything else, although farming on Apache lands was difficult. Furthermore, the Apache reservations were rich in natural resources but the Apaches did not have the skills to become timber jacks, or railroad workers, or dairy farmers, etc. The federal government also had laws that prevented the Indian tribes from developing their natural resources. Unable to sustain themselves, the Apache Indians became dependent on government rations for their living.

All Apache tribal economies have long relied upon the use of the tribe's natural resources as the major source of revenue and employment. Harvesting oil, gas, and timber; ranching; tourism; and hunting and fishing are the cornerstone of the tribal economy. Tribal lands contain abundant sources of woodlands, water sources, minerals, oil, gas, and wildlife. The tribes have utilized these resources well in order to promote a self-sustaining economy.

CONTEMPORARY ISSUES

There are a series of contemporary social, economic, and cultural issues that have deep roots in the history of relations between the Apache tribes and the federal government and its policies. These interrelated issues have touched the heart of the future survival of the Apaches as a distinct people and as Indian tribes. At the center of these issues is the question of whether Apache people will honor their cultural traditions with respect to restoring the family to its rightful position and role in their contemporary societies, or allow the family unit to continue to erode in the face of modern times and circumstances. Tied to this question is whether or not Apache tribes, as legal entities, will exist in the future if they continue to use blood quantum for defining tribal membership and who is or is not an Apache. The breakdown of the family structure and its effects are clearly evident in the rising crime rates related to the use of methamphetamine, the high suicide rates, and critical health issues like the high rates of obesity and diabetes. The Apache people have come to a crossroad where their critical choices and decisions surrounding the interrelated issues will determine their future.

Survival, resiliency, and determination have been cornerstones in Apache character that have brought them through hard times and have crowned their progress and achievements. Although faced with critical issues, they have tackled their problems with determination and commitment. It is their resolve to save their language, eradicate the problems of meth and suicide, and protect their culture and environment. The realization that they are ultimately and totally responsible for their future will serve them well. They have the means to be truly self-determined, but will have to continue to partner with the federal government and maintain the historical trust relationship in order to achieve this goal.

Notes

1. Keith Basso, "Western Apache," in *Southwest*, vol 10 of *Handbook of North American Indians*, volume ed. Alfonso Ortiz (Washington, D.C.: Smithsonian Institution Press, 1983), 463.

2. Veronica E. Tiller, compiler, *Tiller's Guide to Indian Country: Economic Profiles of American Indian Reservations* (Albuquerque: BowArrow Publishing Company, 2005), 354.

3. Ibid., 298.

4. Eve Ball, with Nora Henn and Lynda Sanchez, *Indeh: An Apache Odyssey* (Provo: Brigham Young University Press, 1982), 183–193.

5. Morris E. Opler, "Mescalero Apache," in *Southwest*, vol 10 of *Handbook of North American Indians*, volume ed. Alfonso Ortiz (Washington, D.C.: Smithsonian Institution Press, 1983), 419.

6. Robert W. Young, "Apachean Languages," in *Southwest*, vol 10 of *Handbook of North American Indians*, volume ed. Alfonso Ortiz (Washington, D.C.: Smithsonian Institution Press, 1983), 393–400.

7. Portions of pages 8 to 11 were previously published in Semos Unlimited, *Nuevo Mexico: An Anthology of History*, Las Vegas: New Mexico Highlands University, 2009. Reprinted with permission.

8. Ibid., 58–59.

9. Basso, "Western Apache," 466.

10. Ibid.

11. *Tiller's Guide*, 298.

12. Ibid., 347.

13. *Tiller's Guide*, 289.

14. Ibid.

15. For detailed accounts of the Apache Wars, see: Dan L. Thrapp, *The Conquest of Apacheria* (Norman: University of Oklahoma Press, 1967); *Victorio and the Mimbres Apaches* (Norman: University of Oklahoma Press, 1974); Robert M. Utley, *Frontier Regulars: The United States Army and the Indian, 1866–1891* (Bloomington: Indiana University Press, 1973).

16. Morris E. Opler, "Chiricahua Apache," in *Southwest*, vol 10 of *Handbook of North American Indians*, volume ed. Alfonso Ortiz (Washington, D.C.: Smithsonian Institution Press, 1983), 407–409; John Anthony Turcheneske, Jr., "The United States Congress and the Release of the Apache Prisoners of War at Fort Sill," *Chronicles of Oklahoma* 54:1 (1976): 200–226.

2

Apache Religion and Worldviews

THIS CHAPTER will provide a general overview of traditional Apache religion, its main tenets and principles, and how it is the foundation for the world-views about living in harmony and in balance with all of nature. Several Apache Creation stories and ceremonies will illustrate how Apache people explain their origins and their relationship with the universe, and how they pray and give thanks. The impact of Apache religion and worldview on the historical use and occupancy of tribal lands will also be explained. The survival of traditional Apache religion and its suppression, as well as the religious practices on Apache reservations in contemporary times, will be discussed.

The basic religion of the Apache people is Southern Athapaskan in origin, so there are many foundational similarities between the Navajo and Apache religions, especially in their basic tenets and concepts. However, there are also strong differences between the Navajo and Apache, as reflected in the religious practices and customs among both the Western Apaches and the Eastern Apaches. This discussion will focus on the practices among the modern-day Eastern and Western Apaches of Arizona, New Mexico, and Oklahoma.

Native American religions, including the Apache Indians', have been a topic of keen interest to non-Indians from serious scholars to popular fiction writers and filmmakers. The interpretations have run the gamut from the portrayal of Apache religion as a paganistic and demonic cult to reflective and genuinely intellectual. Even Apaches themselves have had differing views of their religion and how it should be portrayed, discussed, and shared with the rest of the world.

Americans began moving onto Apache lands in New Mexico and Arizona in the late 1800s, and travel accounts became the major source of information on Apache life for the U.S. public. One of the earliest firsthand accounts of Apaches reenforced the existing negative image of the Apache. It stated that, "the Apache has become the most treacherous, blood-thirsty, villainous and unmitigated rascal upon earth [. . .] incapable of improvement. . . . "[1] This popular image of the Apache went from bad to worse as the desire for Apache country increased and movement onto their lands intensified, which eventually led to the Apache Wars of the late nineteenth century. The view of the religion of the Apaches went hand in hand with the perception of their character as a people. During the 1880s, it was the federal Indian policy that all Native Americans be assimilated into U.S. society, and at the forefront of the assimilation policy was a direct assault on their religion.

It was not until the first part of the twentieth century that scholars, especially anthropologists, ethnologists, and linguists, began to seriously study the culture and religion of the Apache people in an attempt to understand them in light of the largely unsuccessful assimilation efforts that were leading to their extinction. The predominant scholarly works among the Apaches were conducted beginning in the 1930s, primarily by two anthropologists, Morris Opler and Keith Basso, and several linguists, James Mooney, Pliny Goddard, and Harry Hoijer. The views and interpretations of Apache religion in existing literature are formulated by these scholars. In addition there are numerous historians and writers who have produced works on Apaches, but mostly on the Apache Wars, federal Indian policies, and a spattering of tribal histories.

In the 1950s, Eve Ball, a writer from New Mexico, had the rare opportunity to interview Asa Daklugie, a Chiricahua Apache, who had elected to make the Mescalero Apache Reservation his home in 1913. In that year a number of Chiricahua Apaches who were prisoners of war and interned at Fort Sill, Oklahoma, chose to join their brethren, the Mescalero Apache, on their reservation. Daklugie was the son of Juh (pronounced Ho), who was Geronimo's brother-in-law and fellow warrior in the Apache Wars of the 1870s and 1880s. Daklugie asserted that understanding the religion was key to understanding the Apache people themselves. He also explained that their religion is something that the Apache people have protected from those who would hope to destroy it. Daklugie made some comparisons between Apache religion and Christianity. He went on to say that,

The Apaches have always believed in one God, whose name is Ussen. The word means Creator of Life. He put the Apache on the land which He had created for us, and He laid down certain laws which we were to obey. These are very much like your Ten Commandments, with the exception of our not being required to observe the Sabbath. Of that we knew nothing [. . .] Your keeping your God locked up in a trap all week and letting him out an hour or two on Sunday is also strange. To us, instead of being our prisoner, Ussen is free and everywhere, always with us. We obey him. You say you do, but your people use profane language. We have too much respect to use it; in our language there is not any profanity.[2]

Daklugie explained that there was not a concept of heaven and hell in the Apache religion. The equivalent of heaven was what he referred to as the "Happy Place," which is beautiful, with animals, nature, loved ones, and safety.[3] Daklugie's account is laced with bitterness and is a natural reaction to how his Apache religion has been treated throughout history. His views can better be understood with a discussion that explains Apache religion from the viewpoint and wisdom of Apache people who have served as informants for non-Indian scholars and writers, and from the studied observation of scholars, both Indian and non-Indian.

APACHE RELIGIONS: BASIC TENETS AND CONCEPTS

All Apache fundamental religious concepts, beliefs, and philosophies are basically the same, but due to physical environments and changing historical circumstances and influences, there are many differences in the application of the concepts and beliefs, especially in the way ceremonial rituals and customs are practiced. The religious differences can be likened to Christianity, in the sense that there are numerous church denominations that place different emphasis on the basic tenets of Christianity.

Apache religion explains the relations between the Supreme Creator, the universe, all living things, and human beings. Apachean religion cannot be separated from the Apache worldview. Religion is based on fundamental beliefs about essential and common assumptions. Religion constitutes the most important body of ideas and worldviews for the Apache tribes. Not all ideas are religious, as is to be expected, but the shared philosophy of life is part of what the community defines as its religious ideas. These beliefs explain the origins of human beings and the order of the universe.

THERE IS NO ONE CREATION NARRATIVE

The Creation story or emergence story of how man and his universe were created is the foundation for the religion of the Apaches. Each tribe, and even groups within a tribe, has their own versions. There is no one version that is the "truth" or the dominant version, but within the tribal variations, there are common themes. The Apache worldview is expressed by "a cycle of rich and intricate stories that teach concepts about, and explain, the creation of the universe and the sequences of stages by which it reached its present form."[4] These religious concepts, together with those comprising the origins of ceremonies and supernatural powers, are considered sacred by the Apaches. The Creation stories are also told for various other reasons, including the preservation of tribal history and for social and instructional purposes.

The Mescalero Apache version is one example of the Apache Creation story. It has all the fundamental Apache religious beliefs about the universe, the creation of man and animals, and the relationship between man, animals, and the environment. It tells of the proper role of all living beings and how they are to keep a balance in the universe, and finally, when there is an imbalance, how to restore the balance through prayer, songs, and ceremonies.

The following summarized Creation story is based on Bernard Second's account. Second was a Mescalero Apache spiritual leader who served as an informant for Claire R. Farrer, an ethnoastronomer.[5] According to Second, at the beginning of time there was nothing except for the Eternal Power or the Great Spirit, who will be referred to as "He" in this discussion. (In Apache religion it cannot be assumed that the male is more powerful or more important than the female.) He decided that He would create, so on the first day He created the celestial and sacred beings: the Sun, Mother Earth, the Moon, the Stars, the Wind, and the Rainbow. On the second day He created the animal kingdom; all variety of animals that crawl and fly, like reptiles, worms, insects, and birds. On the third day He created the four-legged of the world, like the buffalo, deer, elk, antelope, the horse, and all creatures that walk with hair on their bodies. On the fourth day, He created man: the Apaches.[6]

At creation time, the Great Spirit decreed that Man was the weak and fragile relative and instructed all his creation to help Man live in the world. The Sun was appointed as his representative and was told that, "You will be that which Man sees." The Moon was to be Man's eyesight at night. When Man traveled at night, the Stars would provide direction and guidance. The Wind was to "carry Man's word." (So an Apache person always has to be careful what they say on a windy day.) Rainbow was always to remind Man of the beauty of all his creation.[7]

All animals were given certain guidance with regard to their duties to Man. The sacred bond or symbiotic relationship between Man and animals was defined. To the Apaches, all animals are still considered sacred beings to be treated with respect, and there are some special animals that are to be held in veneration.

The top of the animal hierarchy was Eagle, endowed by the Creator as allknowing, and the holy symbol for Man's authority in spiritual, political, and social matters. The Eagle represented Man's civil authority, so that when man wore eagle feathers, everyone knew that mankind was given autonomy to live as a people.[8] The image of Indian chiefs wearing eagle feather bonnets to symbolize their leadership positions is common, as well as warriors wearing war bonnets usually made from eagle feathers.

THE ROLE OF ANIMALS

The Buffalo, *iyane* (an Apache word that connotes "eater," because it always spends the day eating and grazing), was told, "you will be your weak relative's food, lodging, and clothing."[9] The Elk and Deer were told that they too would provide food and clothing for Man. These animals graciously accepted their roles. When the Antelope was given his instruction, he replied, "If I am to be eaten by them, if they eat even one hair of my body, it will kill them."[10] For his lack of generosity, Antelope was given the sentence that "your curiosity will be your undoing."[11]

There are also animals that were assigned duties and characteristics that made them messengers of bad news and omens, like the Owl, and the Snake, who is to be avoided. Snakes carry illnesses and are considered omens for bad luck. In the Mescalero version of the Creation story, the Owl was told, "You are My messenger. So you will be Man's messenger."[12] For the Jicarilla Apache, the Bear is considered a sacred animal in charge of healing man and a special ceremony known as the Bear Dance is conducted by when someone gets sick from various afflictions associated with the bear or snake.

Of all the animals, the Coyote was given a role that defined the character of mankind, exemplifying all the strengths and weaknesses, from the admirable and pathetic to the dignified and ridiculous.[13] Specifically, he was told, "All of Man's weaknesses and foolishness you will carry—so that Man will not be alone in his foolishness and weaknesses. And that you will wander on this Earth and in the night you will cry in your foolishness, even though nothing bothers you, as Man will."[14] It was Coyote who had a dual role of teaching the people about how to make a living and teaching moral lessons through his foolishness.[15] He taught them how to plant, gather and roast mescal, weave baskets, and smoke tobacco. Through Coyote stories people are taught about stealing and telling lies because, in most Coyote stories, his dishonest or foolish behavior leads to visible, and often permanent, consequences. For example, Coyote earned his black tail when it was scorched by Sun as a punishment for trying to steal fire.[16] The Coyote stories are told only in the winter months, and the versions are as endless and as varied as the differences in physical surroundings, beliefs and customs, and histories of the Apache people.

The role and impact of the horse in and on Apache life has been great. The impact it has had is similar to the impact of the automobile on American life.

As related by Bernard Second, the horse was given the role of being the beast of burden. The Horse was told, "You will be the one people boss around." It was decreed that there would be a special bond of love between man and horse, but with it would also come war, sorrow, and hardship.[17]

It is generally believed that the Apaches adopted the horse, which was brought by the Spanish, anywhere between 1541 and the early 1600s, depending on the location and the evidence provided by written records.[18] LaVerne Harrell Clark provides an insight into the how the Lipan Apaches explain their acquisition of the horse. The other Apache versions are quite similar to this one. The Lipan Apaches believe that the deity Killer-of- Enemies created the first horse from a "dazzling array of nature's forces and elements, of plants and artifacts."[19] The spine and legs were formed from corn stalk and "from that time on the skeleton of the horse has been jointed like the stalk of corn."[20] Using a substance that forms on the ground after a heavy rain and resembles soapsuds, he formed the lungs. The horse's kidneys and liver were made from hailstones, as were his teeth. A bolt of lightning was fastened to the inside of the nostrils to give his creation a fiery breath. According to the Lipan:

> He collected rain to form the mane and tail, and he also used rain, along with the rainbow, to form the hoofs. The Lipan say that today we can still see the results of his using the rainbow; it makes the hoofs of some horses—especially white and gray ones—look as though they are tinted. From dew Killer-of-Enemies formed the fetlocks, and unfortunately for mankind, under the hooves he fixed an arrow, which makes a horse's kick very dangerous.
>
> For the completion of his work of art, the culture hero had saved some of his finest resources. For a short while, he borrowed the crescent moon to form the ear, and he took the evening star down from the heavens long enough to make the horse's eye from a piece of it. From these luminaries his horse received the power to see and hear both day and night. Last of all, he gave his creation life. To do this, he drew in a whirlwind from each of the four directions and put them in four different places—one entered the flank, another went under the shoulders, and the remaining two penetrated the hips on either side. When the winds entered its body, the Lipan Apache's first mythical horse began to breathe and move, and Killer-of-Enemies had himself a fine stallion to ride from that time on.[21]

This was how the horse was created. It was the Spanish who brought the Apaches the physical horse, but it was they who created the possibility of the horse in their minds and through their sacred prayers and their deities brought it to them.

According to the worldview of the Apache, after the four days of Creation, the ancestral people emerged from the underworld. The various Apache versions of the emergence also share themes and concepts. The differences in the stories are found in the locations or places associated with the emergence (usually within the particular homelands of the various Apache tribes), the names given to the first man and woman, the sequence of events, the deities, and certain attributes of the deities.

The commonalities are that the Apaches originated from Mother Earth and Father Sun, whose offspring were two twin warriors. Upon emergence, the ancestral deities were faced with strife and conflict and the offspring, who were known by various names (Monster Slayer, Killer-of-Enemies, or He Kills on Earth), made the world safe for human habitation, and eventually the people moved south to their new homelands.

The Mescalero Apache version, according to Bernard Second, begins with their original site of emergence in the Land of Ever Winter. They call this place the Home of Winter, on the shores of the big lake called, Water That You Cannot See Over.[22] It was on the shores of this lake that Mother Earth bore twins: He Killed On Earth and He Was Born For Water. She raised them on the banks of the lake under warm rocks, nursing them until they became men. Mother Earth and Father Sun made wives for them. The Twin Brothers became the ancestral fathers of all the Apaches. At this time, all the animals of the world talked the same language as the people, and it was a good world. Then something went wrong and the people began to have enemies. The first twin destroyed all the unpleasant things of this world and made the earth beautiful, good, and safe for the people. The second twin, He Was Born For Water, made available all the foods of this world. The people lived surrounded by beauty and goodness, but something lured them in a southerly direction. The Twin Brothers told them to go forth as a people, and soon the people left their place of origin. The people were forewarned that in their new lives and on the new lands, they would encounter heartache, lonesomeness, and war and brutality, but there would also be happiness. When they encountered difficulties, all they had to do was call on the Twin Brothers, and to have faith that they would be protected. They promised that they would one day return and deliver them. In the new land they were to call themselves, ^{n}dé, the People.[23]

The various Apache Creation or emergence stories are quite complicated in that there are a multitude of characters and different tribes emphasize the role of various sacred beings depending on what message they want relay. In the Western Apache version, the People also emerged from beneath the earth and encountered wicked creatures that devoured them and stole their women. A young maiden, Changing Woman, gave birth to twin sons; one was the son of Sun and the other was the son of Black Water. In this version, the first twin, Slayer of Monsters, returned to the home of his father, who refused to acknowledge him as his son and forced him to undergo a series of tests. Slayer of Monsters accomplished his tests with the help of sacred ancestral animals like Spider Woman, Fly, and Gopher. Father Sun was satisfied and sent Slayer of Monsters back to earth to teach the People how to dress in proper Apache clothing, and how to use bows and arrows and horses. Slayer of Monsters, with the Son of Black Water, killed the evil creatures and made the world safe for humans.[24]

In the Jicarilla Apache Creation story, the emergence from the underworld is similar to the other Apache accounts, but it is different with regard to the names of the sacred beings and location of emergence. In the Jicarilla version, Wind offered to roll back the waters in four directions to form the oceans. In his zealousness, He dried up all the waters, leaving nothing for the living creatures to drink. Prayers were offered and soon, rivers, lakes, and streams appeared. The people discovered that the earth was inhabited by monsters, which were later killed by Monster Slayer. With the help of the other sacred beings, all obstacles that made the earth an unsafe place were eliminated.

After the Jicarillas came to this world, they were given elaborate laws, customs, traditions, and more ceremonies that were to be observed forever. At this time, all the human attributes that the animals possessed were taken from them, though they were allowed to retain the powers they had to facilitate the emergence from the underworld. For this reason, the Jicarillas, like the other Apaches, are never to abuse, molest, or mistreat animals. If an animal is hunted for food, proper prayers and rituals are to be performed. Plants and mineral life are also to be respected since they too possess supernatural attributes, as healing properties and as food.[25]

All natural and living objects in the Apache universe, including man, are personifications of the Creator. Through ritual, his powers can be used for human purposes. For that reason, the more important sources of His powers—Sun, Moon, Wind, and Lightning—are always represented in the ceremonies. Within this framework, a pantheon of good and evil supernatural energies are also recognized. The Apache are made aware that this world consists of both good and evil and that man is not a perfect creature, but one with natural and deep blemishes in his basic character.

THE FOUR CARDINAL DIRECTIONS

The sanctity of the number four, as represented by the four cardinal directions (east, south, west, and north) is key to understanding Apache religion. The universe was created in four days and anchored by the four cardinal directions. There are four seasons: spring, summer, fall, and winter. All creation is represented by a specific direction to define its character, elements, and qualities. Sun resides in the easterly direction because the order of original creation started with the sun, so the first and opening prayer offered in any ceremony begins with an offering in this direction. In prayers and ceremonies, pollen from a plant native to a specific region is offered to all four directions, starting with the east. Going clockwise, the other celestial bodies also represent a certain direction, with the moon for south; the wind, thunder, and lightning for the west; and the rainbow for the north.[26]

Cardinal directions are defined by their color elements, but vary from tribe to tribe. Basically, the four sacred colors are sunrise/sunray white or white like the snow-capped mountains for the east; blue-green or turquoise for the south; sunset yellow, like the hue when the sun hits the beige sandstone hills, for the west; and the dark blue-black of the night sky for the north.[27] Symbolically, the animals that figure prominently into the Creation stories are also associated with one of the cardinal directions: Buffalo with east, Elk with south, Deer with west, and Antelope with north.[28]

THE ROLE OF THE SACRED APACHE LANDS

The Creation stories set the foundation for the religion of the Apaches and define their sacred lands, which are usually delineated by four sacred mountains and rivers. The lands have a significance that goes deep to the heart and soul of the people. The sacred Apache homelands have shaped their religion, culture, lifestyles, and their very identities as a distinct people for countless generations. The land has permanency, longevity, and it is endless, enduring, and stable. It is the space where they have safeguarded their religion, stories and traditions, and ideals that have influenced their perception and behavior. Geographical features have served as markers of the past because they have endured through time. It has allowed them to relate all historical events within the confines of their lands.[29] As one historian has noted, "for what matters to the Apaches is where events occurred, not when...."[30] " ... [I]n contradistinction to Western emphasis on precisely when events happened in historical time, native cultures more often emphasize and focus their concern on where an event took place. It is the occupancy of tribal lands that tie them to their lands. It is from the land that they understand the structure of their ceremonies and the place from where they communicate with the spirits and their Creator."[31] The Apaches do not extend their religious beliefs and traditions beyond the borders of their sacred lands. Their beliefs are for them and them alone. For this reason, one would not find an Apache trying to convert another person to their religion.

The persistence of Apache culture, in a real sense, is connected to their land and environment. The land not only holds the key to their past but defines their present. In thought and action, the Apaches live by the dictates of their physical surroundings. The features of the landscape are instrumental in the ongoing development and realization of their modern-day cultures.

Native American Views on Ownership of Land

The Apache relationship to their sacred lands has impacted their concept of land ownership. Prior to colonization, the concept of land ownership was foreign to them. The Apaches saw their lands as a sacred space and place given to them by the Creator. The land offered them natural resources and wildlife. By custom, the land was there for their people to share and use to make a living and to be treated in a respectful and reverential manner. As far as the Apache were concerned, no one had the right to sell their land, not the chief, headmen, warriors, or even the elders. Their view became a point of contention with the Euro-Americans who invaded their lands. They fought so hard to remain on it and when they could not, the impact was devastating.

For example, when the earth was made inhabitable, the Jicarilla Apache people traveled in all four directions, finally settling in what, to them, was the epicenter of the earth. The Creator chose four sacred rivers to define the boundaries of their country: the Arkansas River in southern Colorado, the Canadian, Rio Grande, and Pecos Rivers in New Mexico. This land became the holy land for the Jicarilla Apaches. Within this territory are also various mountain ranges and peaks that are considered sacred. When the Jicarillas were relocated to their current reservation in north-central New Mexico in 1887, the impact was spiritually and physically devastating. By the 1920s, it was evident that the Jicarilla Apache would become extinct within several generations if something were not done about the high number of deaths due to tuberculosis, trachoma, and other diseases.[32]

The other Apache tribes also have sacred mountains within their reservations. For the Mescalero Apaches they are the Sierra Blanca, Guadalupe, Three Sisters Mountain, and the Oscura Mountain.[33] Often the Capitan and San Agustin mountains, and Salinas Peak are also included.[34]

Ceremonial Practices among the Apache Tribes

The contemporary Apache tribes of Arizona and New Mexico share in common the Puberty Feast. The Mountain Spirit or Gah Dances or ceremonies are held on the White Mountain, San Carlos, and Mescalero Apache reservations, as well as on a limited basis at Fort Sill, Oklahoma. Only the Jicarilla Apaches of northern New Mexico have the ceremonial relay races and the Bear Dances. All Apache tribes have various types of healing and prayer-type ceremonials that are often personal and/or family-oriented.

CEREMONIAL RITES: THE PUBERTY FEAST

The religious ceremony that is actively carried out today by all Apache tribes and that has been conducted by all Apache people since time immemorial is known by several names: the puberty feast, the initiation feast, the adolescence rites, puberty rites, and the coming-out feast. The term Puberty Feast will be used in this discussion. This four-day ceremony, representing the four days of Creation, focuses on young teenage girls when they start their menstrual cycle. It is a re-creation of the origin ceremony held for White Painted Woman or Changing Woman, the supreme female sacred being, during the creation of mankind. The physical transformation from adolescence to adulthood is a time of celebration in recognition of a girl who has started the journey to becoming an adult. It especially celebrates the role of the female in all its forms and manifestations as acknowledged in the Creation stories and as intended by the Creator. This ceremony recognizes the female forces in the supreme and sacred equation to balance all life and energy forces for all time. It dictates that neither the male nor female is better, stronger, smarter, or more important than the other.[35] During the ceremony, the young girl is initiated into her new role as a person who gives life through birth, who is responsible for her children, and who has a myriad of duties and responsibilities as a valuable member of her family, her clan, her band, her tribe, and her marriage, if she chooses to get married.

Preparation for the Ceremony

Once a young girl starts her menstruation cycle she informs her mother or other female member of her family. The mother or head of household hires a medicine person to lead a four-day ceremony. The ceremony takes place so that the last or fourth night corresponds with the full moon. The medicine person can select to invite other medicine people to assist with the ceremony, to have apprentices present, and even to have a group of assistants. Preparation for the feast or celebration begins with finding the food resources, lining up the manpower for the service of food, setting up the camp and ceremonial tepee, collecting the necessary ceremonial items, and making the announcements and issuing invitations. Any person or group of persons in charge of these activities are highly skilled individuals with leadership and management skills, with the ability to manage and organize people and resources, and with a strong commitment to carrying out the mission of the ceremony. They are essentially the ceremonial support team.

How the Ceremony Is Conducted

The main ceremonial activity is conducted in the ceremonial tepee that faces east. The four main tepee poles are called, by the Mescalero Apache, the Four Grandfathers. Each one stands for a day of Creation and each one represents one of the four cardinal directions.[36] During the ceremony, the head medicine man sings scores of sacred songs that recount the Creation stories and songs that ask from the Creator blessings for a long, happy, and productive life for the girl and her family. On the first night the ceremony usually ends at 11 p.m. and on the last night the ceremony ends with sunrise. The position of stars and constellations guides the head medicine person and the troupe of singers throughout the four nights. The singers observe the movement of the Big Dipper, beginning with its first appearance in the west and south until it sets behind the north in the early morning before dawn.[37]

THE WESTERN APACHE CEREMONY

While the Puberty Feast serves as a ceremonial common denominator among the Apache tribes today, there are major differences in the way it is conducted. The Western Apaches conduct the ceremony usually as a group event whereby all the young girls participate. In addition, the Mountain Spirit Dancers are a part of the ceremony. For the Mescalero Apache, this ceremony has become an annual and public event held on the Fourth of July. When the Apaches were first placed on their reservations in the 1880s, the U.S. government policy was to end the "pagan religious practices," and the staging of these puberty ceremonies was not only discouraged but outlawed. Later, when tolerance returned, the ceremony was conducted as one event. Lack of economic resources made it more feasible to make the event a joint and public event, rather than as an individual event as in the past.

THE JICARILLA APACHE PUBERTY FEAST OR "KEESTA"

Among the Jicarilla Apache, the puberty feast, or "Keesta" as it is called in the Jicarilla language, is still an individual event, although on rare occasions several girls may participate together. One reason that the Jicarilla puberty ceremony is often referred to in the scholarly literature as the adolescence ceremony is because the girl has a teenage boy or young adult male as her partner.[38]

The Jicarilla Keesta involves telling the Creation stories, performing the songs and prayers of the main religious doctrines, presenting the moral teachings of the Jicarilla people, and offering prayers for future prosperity, happiness, and a balanced and harmonious life. This rite of passage celebrates the role of women in Jicarilla society. It conveys the idea that men and women

San Carlos Apache Sunrise Ceremony, Apache women watching the Mountain Spirit Dancers. (Courtesy of Sheldon Nunez-Velarde, Jicarilla Apache)

are equally important, that one cannot exist without the other. At the Keesta, the girl is given instruction ranging from the universal to the mundane, including the everyday norms of behavior. During the ceremony, the young girl and boy are taught how to manage their sexuality, in that they are taught not to be ashamed of it but to recognize that all life is about renewal, reproduction, and seasonal cycles and change. Because sexuality is one of the main sources of conflict in personal relationships, this ceremony addresses the issue directly. The Keesta teaches the young people to fully and openly accept their human nature in all its dimensions and, in that way, learn to live their adult lives in a balanced manner.

Furthermore, the young girl and boy are taught that if they can reach their spiritual consciousness through prayer, they can do anything they want in life; that they can manage all aspects of their lives. The girl is specifically told that she will learn to manage her life, including the pain of childbirth, her love affairs, and her relationship with the world.

The Keesta rituals have been developed to signify the goodness of entering adulthood. For example, when the grandmother bestows the gift of womanhood to her granddaughter, she tells her, "You have been given a gift from the Creator;

you have become a woman, and being a woman you are blessed." Another ritual aspect is giving certain objects, such as a blanket, that symbolize the significance of women's roles in nurturing a family. It is this blanket that the woman takes to wrap her babies in celebration of their births; it is what she uses to swaddle a sick child; it is the object that she uses when she dances and celebrates.[39]

The young girl is traditionally attended almost full-time during the four ceremonial days by a wise woman whose job it is to inculcate her with the wisdom of the ages, with advice such as "always remember to be generous," "never reject children in any way, especially by physically pushing them away from you," and "always be careful of what you say." The latter relates to one of the most basic principles of Jicarilla religion, since at the beginning of time, "the truth was spoken, and so it was." In everyday life, thought and its manifestation through the spoken word are very potent, and people must be careful in what they think and say.

The young boy's uncles or other elderly males teach him about how to love all his people. One role of the man in Jicarilla society is to provide leadership for his people, and to be a leader a man must have compassion for children and old people and respect for social order. This is one of the lessons that he is taught.

The ceremony represents not only a celebration but the girl's family's generosity, and demonstrates and reinforces the Apache custom of giving and receiving. It is also another symbolic way to reinforce the ever-present family unity and the idea of helping each other. In the days when dire economic poverty plagued the Jicarilla people, it was almost impossible to have a Keesta without the help and cooperation of the entire extended family and friends.

MOUNTAIN SPIRIT DANCERS OR GAH DANCERS

Among the Western Apache tribes, the Mountain Spirit Dancers or Gah Dancers conduct various types of ceremonies. The Mountain Spirit Dancers are also called Crown Dancers, and these terms will be used interchangeably in this discussion. The purposes of the ceremonies are to conduct either a blessing or healing ceremony, or both, when requested by members of the tribe. A blessing or healing ceremony can range from an individual request, to the tribal government's request to bless a new building during a grand opening. Often, a ceremony is a combined blessing and healing ceremony and it can take place anytime of the year.

To access the power of life and the powers of creation, the Mountain Spirit Dancers undergo a transformation where they become the embodiment of the four sacred directions. From their preparation in the ceremonial tepee to the time they remove their masks on the last night, they are no longer humans or anthropomorphic deities, but the reincarnation of the spiritual

San Carlos Apache Mountain Spirit Dancers. (Courtesy of Sheldon Nunez-Velarde, Jicarilla Apache)

powers of life. They access the power inherent in the process of the predictability of natural forces, like how the celestial bodies work together so that the sun always rises in the east and sets in the west and day is followed by night.[40] Transformation is enhanced with prayers and songs. The four directions are a literal and symbolic system that represent the process of growth, life, and change, which is what the dancers become.[41] Songs are understood to manifest power and are often likened to prayers.

The Crown Dancers dance around a ceremonial fire. To a tourist or outsider, they may appear as grotesque figures that charge into the flames and thrust their staves at each other as they seemingly compete for the crowd's attention, but there is much more to their dancing.[42] The Crown Dancers must always follow each other in the prescribed order of the four directions of east, south, west, and north. Their ceremonial dress is replete with abstract and formal symbolism related to the power of the four directions. Operating as a unit, every action and movement is done in precise patterns that are synchronized to reflect how the four directions are always regular and predictable. It is through their regularity that power is manifested and channeled through their bodies and actions.[43]

The Role of the Sacred Clowns

Standing in line behind the Crown Dancers are clowns, whose role in the ceremony appears enigmatic or odd, until one understands it. In comparison to the Crown Dancers, who always act collectively in their performance of the dances, the clowns are not bound by any formal rules; they do what they want to do, from the absurd and crazy to the odd and humorous. They are the complete opposite of predictability and following the rules.[44] During the ceremony, the clowns can mock the dancers, go in and out of the dance grounds, dance with the women and carry a cowbell and wear tennis shoes and gunny sacks. The outward physical appearance of the clowns and their outfits is entirely intentional.[45]

Ironically, the spiritual power of the clowns involves having all the power of the four directions simultaneously. The Crown Dancers only have the power of all four directions when they function as a complete and integrated unit. Such is not the case for the clowns. They manifest power of all four directions independent of other clowns.[46] Unlike the Crown Dancers, what the clowns physically represent is not explicitly encoded in the symbolism that is used on their bodies or on their outfits. They are clumsy and imprecise, often making mistakes, yet are the most powerful. They are the power of humanity, the power of the human mind. What they point out is that humans are often unpredictable and inconsistent.[47] The clowns represent the fact that humans have agency over their lives, can make right and wrong choices, and do not always reflect the precision, predictability, and unity as represented by the Crown Dancers. The ceremonies involving the Crown and Clown dancers reflect the Mescaleros belief in an individual's responsibility to culture and tradition, and to living a meaningful life.[48]

THE JICARILLA APACHE CEREMONIES: THE BEAR DANCE

In addition to the Keesta, the Jicarilla Apache also have two other ceremonies, the purpose of which is similar to those of the Western Apache ceremonies: for blessings and healings. The Bear Dance, also known as the Holiness Rites, is a four-day ceremony. It takes place in a large circular structure made of pine, spruce, or piñon with an opening to the east. This structure is big enough to accommodate as many as six large fires and up to 300 people. Inside this structure is the tepee where the medicine people (either men or women or both) pray and sing for the patients and all members assembled. Twelve sacred clowns (*Cha'sh jini*) and twelve sacred beings (*T'a nati*), make their appearances only the fourth night during the full moon to help cure a patient or patients afflicted or suffering from illnesses symbolically caused by Bear, Snake, or those caused by Wind or Fire. This healing ceremony gets its spiritual sanction from time of emergence when two young girls were rescued from an unnamed danger and returned to the people. Like the clowns of the Mountain Spirit Dancers, the *Cha'sh jini* are "licensed" to be humorous in their actions and to say outrageous things. It is to them that tribal members can go for blessings and prayers outside the structure. The *T'a nati* are serious, reserved, and work as a unit. On the fifth morning, the ceremony ends with the "shaking of blankets" and a race back to the structure for final prayers.

THE JICARILLA APACHE CEREMONIAL RELAY RACE

The other ceremony conducted by the Jicarilla Apache is the Ceremonial Relay Race that takes place every September 14 and 15 no matter what day of the week these dates occur. This event is a huge tribal camp-out at Stone Lake on the northern part of the reservation. It is equivalent to an annual family reunion for all families. It is the event that brings off-reservation Apache tribal members home. The race is between the two clans, the Olleros and the Llaneros, and it is the ceremony that highlights the young adolescent boys. The ceremony is carried out in a circular structure made from tall

Jicarilla Apache Women from White Clan dancing on track prior to ceremonial relay race. (Courtesy of Dina Velarde)

young cottonwood trees, but the race is on an east-west track. It derives its rationale from the emergence story, when there was a race between the Sun and the Moon. The Sun and Moon enlisted the aid of the cultural heroes and all sacred beings and animals. This race reflected the duality of the food resources for the People, who were primarily hunters and gatherers. It was deemed that there would be more plants or animals available for food depending on which clan won the race that year. This ceremony is to take place every year without fail.

WOMEN IN RELIGION

As a rule, women do not carry out the role of the sacred beings in the ceremonies for the Jicarilla Apache Bear Dance, or as Mountain Spirit Crown Dancers for the Western Apache. Only men serve in those roles. For all other types of healing ceremonies, and the puberty feasts, women can be medicine people. Women have a large role in the puberty feasts, from which they may learn the ritual language and the sacred songs and prayers. They can then pass what they have learned to others.[49]

Clan runners from White Clan at Go jii Ya in 2009. (Courtesy of Dina Velarde)

SUMMARY OF RELIGIOUS CONCEPTS, PHILOSOPHIES, AND TENETS

In the collective Apache Creation stories, the world order was created in four days, giving the number four a powerful attribute. Reinforcing its power are the four cardinal directions. The Sun and Mother Earth are physical manifestations of the Creator and are responsible for life and upon whom all life depends. The Apache understand that people do not and cannot exist without the energy forces like the sun, wind, moon, rain, and the natural phenomena created by these energy forces.[50]

All living creatures are totally dependent upon all other creations for their existence. In this sacred hierarchy, people are inherently weak, because they require the entirety of creation for their lives.[51] A balance exists when everything maintains its proper place and order according to the divine plan; when something is upset within the rightness of the universe, it becomes necessary to restore the balance and harmony and ceremonies must be performed. "Living with the sacred for the Apache means living in balance with the spiritual and physical worlds. It means having a 'good heart' and walking a 'good path.'"[52] It is about living with the sacred in every moment, having gratitude, and recognizing the sacred and mysterious powers in all things. Such practices do not lead to salvation or everlasting life, or transcendence from the mundane, but to true appreciation of the wonder and mystery of the universe and life itself. It is the here and now that is important, not the ever after or the great beyond.[53]

THE SUPPRESSION OF THE APACHE RELIGION

Throughout U.S. history, Native American religions have been viewed as illegitimate, paganistic, and even sacrilegious. By the late 1800s it became the policy of the federal government to suppress the religion of the Apaches as a way to assimilate them into the dominant society. It was the position of the federal government, with the full support of the established U.S. Christian churches, that the Apaches forego their native religion and customs in favor of becoming full-fledged U.S. farmers and Christians.

Ironically, one of the major reasons for the colonization of the Americas was for the European people to pursue religious freedom, yet they practiced the same religious intolerance that they themselves were attempting to escape. The guarantee of religious freedom was not extended to Native people. Although the intention of the Euro-Americans may have been good and hopeful that Native Americans would become U.S. citizens, efforts to assimilate were made with or without their permission. In the Apaches' case, everything was done to keep the Apaches from practicing their religion, from separating the children from their parents under threat of starvation and jail to outlawing religious freedom. The chapter on education will discuss the suppression of Apache culture in greater detail. Fortunately for the Apache people, they remained within their native lands, and through their physical isolation they were able to practice their religion, often in secrecy and almost as an underground activity.

In large part, the dominant society has succeeded in suppressing the Apache religion. The suppression of the language has been the most effective means for the decreasing number of Apache people who practice their native religion. Without an understanding of the language it is difficult to participate in the religious ceremonies; however, it has not stopped many Apache people from participating in their native ceremonies.

Today, the majority of Apache tribal members belong to the various Christian sects, like the Dutch Reformed Church; the Catholic Church; the Baptist, Lutheran, Presbyterian denominations; and the Church of Latter Day Saints. The large number of Apache people who are members of the churches cannot be attributed totally to the suppression of traditional religion, as Apache people do have a choice in selecting how they want to worship. Since the acceptance of religion by Apache people comes naturally, many Apache people attend church as well as attend tribal religious activities. But like all Americans who live in a modern society with technology, they have been affected by the mass media. Watching television, surfing the Internet, listening to favorite songs on an iPod, and all facets U.S. life are present in Apache Indian reservation and off-reservation communities. The Apache religion has to compete with all these issues.

INDIAN FREEDOM OF RELIGION ACT OF 1978

In 1978, the Congress of the United States passed the Indian Freedom of Religion Act, which guarantees Native Americans the constitutional right to worship as they please. But, since the Civil Rights movement during the 1960s, there has been a renewed interest in the Apache religion. The best indicator of the interest in Apache religion has been the increase in the number of young Apache girls who have participated in the puberty feasts despite their lack of understanding of the language. On the Jicarilla Apache Reservation, there has also been a renewed interest in the young boys participating in the ceremonial relay race. The revival has been attributed to self-determination policies, the increase in the level of education among the Apache population, and a grass-roots movement in Indian communities that has led to having pride in being Apache. Today, each of the Apache tribes have tribal language programs, have developed tribal dictionaries, and have even developed cultural centers to promote the preservation of their cultures. The restoration of Apache religion is one of the Apache people's goals.

Notes

1. John C. Cremony, *Life Among the Apaches* (San Francisco: A. Roman & Company, 1868), 320.

2. Eve Ball, Nora Henn, and Lynda Sanchez, *Indeh: An Apache Odyssey* (Provo: Brigham Young University Press, 1982), 56.

3. Ibid., 57.

4. Keith Basso, "Western Apache," in *Southwest*, vol. 10 of *Handbook of North American Indians*, volume ed. Alfonso Ortiz (Washington, D.C.: Smithsonian Institution Press, 1983), 477. (Hereinafter cited as Basso, "Western Apache." Basso uses the term *myth* and I have chosen to use *story*. Myth implies it is not true.)

5. Claire R. Farrer, *Living Life's Circle: Mescalero Apache Cosmovision* (Albuquerque: University of New Mexico Press, 1991), 17–26.

6. Ibid., 22–23.

7. Ibid., 23–24.

8. Ibid., 24.

9. Ibid., 24.

10. Ibid., 25.

11. Ibid., 25.

12. Ibid., 26.

13. Basso, "Western Apache," 477.

14. Farrer, *Living Life's Circle*, 26.

15. Basso, "Western Apache," 477.

16. Ibid., 477.

17. Farrer, *Living Life's Circle*, 25–26.

18. LaVerne Harrell Clark, *They Sang for Horses: The Impact of the Horse on Navajo & Apache Folklore* (Boulder: University of Colorado Press, 1966), 1–12.

19. Ibid., 17.

20. Ibid.

21. Ibid., 17–18.

22. Farrer, *Living Life's Circle*, 18.

23. Ibid., 21–22.

24. Basso, "Western Apache," 477.

25. Veronica E. Tiller, *The Jicarilla Apache Tribe: A History* (Albuquerque: BowArrow Publishing Company, 1983), 2–3.

26. Farrer, *Living Life's Circle*, 28–29.

27. Velarde, Lindberg. Telephone Conversation with Author, May 25, 2010.

28. Farrer, *Living Life's Circle*, 29.

29. Martin W. Ball, "Mountain Spirits: Embodying the Sacred in Mescalero Apache Tradition," Ph.D. diss.,University of California, Santa Barbara (Ann Arbor: UMI Dissertation Services, 2000), 41–43.

30. Basso, "Western Apache," 477; Ball, "Mountain Spirits," 44–45.

31. Ball, "Mountain Spirits," 45–46.

32. Tiller, *Jicarilla Apache*, 141–158. Also in Donald E. Worcester, *The Apaches: Eagles of the Southwest* (Norman: University of Oklahoma Press, 1979), 338.

33. H. Henrietta Stockel, *Women of the Apache Nation: Voices of Truth* (Reno: University of Nevada Press, 1991), 55.

34. Ball, "Mountain Spirits," 118–220.

35. Veronica E. Tiller, "Summer," in *Here, Now, and Always: Voices of the First Peoples of the Southwest*, ed. Joan K. O'Donnell (Santa Fe: Museum of New Mexico Press, 2001), 33.

36. Farrer, *Living Life's Circle*, 57.

37. Ibid., 48–57.

38. Morris Opler, "Adolescence Rite of the Jicarilla Apache," *El Palacio*, 49 (1942): 25–38.

39. Veronica E. Tiller, "La Casta, fete de la puberte des Apaches jicarillas", Traduit de l'anglais par Joelle Rostkowski, *Recherches amerindiennes au quebec*, XXX, no. 1, 2000: 27–36.

40. Ball, "Mountain Spirits," 155.

41. Ibid., 158.

42. Ibid., 159.

43. Ibid., 160.

44. Ibid., 162.

45. Ibid., 166.

46. Ibid., 169–170.

47. Ibid., 170.

48. Ibid., 172.

49. Farrer, *Living Life's Circle*, 35–36.

50. Ibid., 27.

51. Ibid.

52. Ball, "Mountain Spirits," 38.

53. Ibid., 38.

3

Language, Art, Music, Dance, and Traditional Dress

HISTORICALLY, the Apache tribes belong to one family known as Southern Athapaskan. Fundamentally, they share in common a religion and a language, although there are variations in the way they are practiced from community to community. Their art, music, song and dance, and even their traditional dress also have more similarities than differences. These cultural arts link their past with the present. Over time, there has been a decline in maintaining their arts due to confinement on Indian reservations and the effects of social disruption and dire economic conditions. Despite such setbacks, the Apache tribal arts and culture have entered a new phase of renewal and revival, and this chapter will discuss that phenomenon.

THE APACHE LANGUAGE GROUPS

There are seven Apachean languages spoken in the Southwest. They consist of the Navajo, Western Apache, Chiricahua, Mescalero, Jicarilla, Lipan, and the Kiowa-Apache.[1] These languages are further divided into the eastern, which consists of the Jicarilla, Lipan, and Kiowa-Apache, and the western, which consists of the Navajo, Western Apache, the Mescalero, and the Chiricahua. These languages are derived from a single ancestral prototype and, dialectically, they are closely related. Apachean speakers from one tribe can understand speakers from another Apache tribe, but not without some difficulty. The Kiowa-Apache is considered a distant Apachean language and will not be addressed in this discussion.

APACHE LANGUAGE SPEAKERS TODAY

Today, the only eastern Apachean language that is still spoken is the Jicarilla Apache language. Less than 30 percent of the population speak it fluently. The age group over 50 years makes up this percentage. The Lipan Apaches as a tribe are nearly extinct, and those descendents that still identify themselves as Lipan live on the Mescalero Apache Reservation and have merged into that tribe and mainly identify themselves as Mescalero Apache. Approximately 30 to 40 percent of Mescalero Apaches still speak their language fluently.[2] On the White Mountain Apache Reservation, the percentage of fluent speakers is 40 percent in the age group of 35 years and older.[3] The highest percentage of fluent Apache speakers is the San Carlos Apache Reservation, where the figure hovers at 50 percent and applies to the age group over 35 years of age.[4]

According to the 2000 U.S. Census, 58.6 percent of Apaches over five years of age on the Fort Apache Reservation spoke the Apache language at home, but only 24.4 percent spoke the language very well. On the San Carlos Reservation, 46.9 percent spoke Apache at home, but only 17.9 spoke the language very fluently.[5] The situation on the Camp Verde and Tonto Apache Reservations is quite different. The population is smaller and the percentages are smaller. What is significant about these percentages is that it does not include the age group under 35. These percentages do not mean that there are no language speakers under the age of 35; it only means that the young people are not learning the language as rapidly as in the past. In effect, it also means that the Apache languages are dying, despite efforts being made by the Apache tribes to have it taught in the schools, at the Cultural Centers, and even in the homes. In Oklahoma, among the Fort Sill Apaches there are no Apache speakers and no concerted efforts are being made for the language's preservation.[6] At the Apache Tribe of Oklahoma, there are about five speakers, who have created language tapes and are working on a language dictionary.[7] The English language is spoken by all Apaches of all ages on all reservations. It is the official language on all the Apache reservations. All business is transacted in the English language.

THE WRITTEN APACHE LANGUAGES

Until recent decades, the Apache language was not a written language, except for the efforts made by several Athapaskan language scholars, including Pliny E. Goddard, James Mooney, Harry Hoijer, and Morris E. Opler.

These scholars created an English phonetic-based alphabet and translated Apache words, phrases, and stories using that system. There was no systematic effort to create an Apache written language until the late 1980s. Today, all Arizona and New Mexico Apache tribes have a written language.

CHARACTERISTICS OF THE APACHE LANGUAGE

It has been very difficult to accurately translate the Apache language into English because, in many instances, there are no equivalents for Apache concepts in the English language. The structure of the language is very different from English and because the language is based on cultural practices and knowledge, it is not conducive to accurate and "across the board" translations. For example, when the English-language concept "The dog is chasing the cat" is translated literally from Apache into English, it is: *dog cat chasing*. In the sentence: "He is chasing after her to be his wife," although the meaning of the word "chasing" is slightly different, it may be used as well. In Apache the word "chasing" in the first sentence has the connotation of hunting and racing, but in the second sentence the word to suggest "chasing" [after her] is entirely different.

The Apache language has a very rich word formation. It is considered a polysynthetic language, meaning that it has a great deal of synthesis and a high degree of fusion within one word. Each word can represent more than one meaning and that one word can have a high degree of blending with other words and their meanings. This also means that the grammatical elements of the language can be obscure and that the parts are not easily distinguishable.[8] As anthropologist and linguist Edward Sapir says, in polysynthetic languages, a "single word expresses either a simple concept or a combination of concepts so interrelated as to form a psychological unity."[9] Two other characteristic features of polysynthetic languages are elaborate noun classification systems and the incorporation of nouns into the verb. For example, the concept "sacred" cannot be defined with just one word in the Apache language, but it becomes overused by scholars and writers in explaining Apache and other Indian religious concepts. One scholar, Martin W. Ball, who worked among the Mescalero Apaches, wrote that attempting to define the word "sacred" defied accurate translation into English, and that any effort to define the word "sacred" should be grounded within a specific Apache tradition. Ball concluded that indigenous words that are translated into English as "sacred" can often be most distinctly translated as "mysterious" or "unknown," which certainly defies definitive translation. To the Mescalero Apaches, he found that sacred could mean "sacred," "medicine," "power," or "mysterious." Ball noted that the word "sacred" was a concept that was not amenable to singular translation or definition and that in some sense, to be true to tradition, the sacred must remain somewhat undefined.[10]

Another scholar, Claire R. Farrer, who also worked among the Mescalero Apaches, found that there was immense importance throughout Apache daily and ritual life in the interplay between sound and silence. In order to hear the voice of the universe, they must listen for the silence. At times, power is manifested through song. By participating in a tribal ceremony, some have the role of voice and others have the role of no voice. At other times the sound/silence alternation is nonvocal, produced by costuming or movement. Proper Apache speech is characterized by periods of quiet—times of no sound and space to listen to the universe in one's own inner voice and contemplate.[11]

Apaches believe that words are so powerful that utterances can create anything. Words can create something good or bad. Children are taught this at a very early age. They are told to watch what they say. If they should say something like someone might die, they are immediately admonished and told to negate what they said by "spitting out" the words. Apaches believe that language was given to them to create their world; so words are their world and they have the power to create with their words.

As in Western societies, there are specialty languages for the various professions, like for the spiritual leaders, medicine men and women, and warriors. In the social sphere, there is also a special way to speak to one's in-laws and even a way to speak about and to one's teasing cousin. (Kinship relationships will be discussed in chapter 5).

THE ORAL TRADITION

Apaches have a strong oral tradition. Oral traditions are the verbal transmission of stories, religious and philosophical knowledge, social values, histories, legends, folktales, folklore, sayings, songs, or chants from one generation of people to the next, who belong to a group and may not have a writing system.

Over the centuries, people who study American Indian cultures have recorded Native knowledge based on their oral traditions. Most of the tribal Creation stories, legends, and folklore that have been translated and written down by scholars and writers are based on these oral traditions. They have been surprised to find consistency between narrations recorded fifty to seventy-five years ago and their rendition today. Scholars attribute the ability to remember and accurately transmit the narrations to the understanding and support provided by the whole group. Indian societies also reinforce the survival of the oral traditions through visual symbols, dances, and songs.[12]

SIGNING OF AGREEMENTS OR TREATIES FOR LAND CESSIONS

Native American societies were based on oral communications, and to a considerable extent they remain so. This oral tradition created many misunderstandings between them and the Europeans, who depended on the written language, especially when it came to the issue of land ownership, its transfer, and sale. Europeans placed little faith in oral commitments. The Indians, on the other hand, derived equally little satisfaction from black scratches on paper. Time and again in the long history of relations between the Apaches and the United States, written agreements for the sale of land were signed by both parties and then violated by the United States. The lack of understanding between the two cultures concerning each others' use of the oral and written communication has perhaps become the heart of interracial conflicts that have led to war, unnecessary suffering, stereotyping, and misunderstandings.

THE SUPPRESSION OF THE APACHE LANGUAGE

After the confinement of the Apaches to reservations, it was the official policy of the federal Indian schools and churches to suppress the speaking of Native languages. There are horror stories about these practices that included public humiliation and corporal punishment. These tactics were effective in deterring young students from using their native languages. Parents were threatened with incarceration and separation from their children if they encouraged their children to speak in their native tongues. This assimilationist practice went hand in hand with the suppression of the practice of Native religions.

Fortunately for the Apaches, who were located far distances from the agency schools and churches, their spoken languages survived the early era of suppression. However, the effect of being told by authoritative figures at institutions in charge of assimilating the Indian children that their native language was the language of pagans, that it denoted backwardness, and that they were not good enough as people because they spoke their native language, was that this message was deeply imprinted on the tribal psyche, and its long-term effects have resulted in lack of self-confidence, the feeling of hopelessness, and the social dysfunction attendant to this type of conditioning.

The suppression of the Apache language contributed to the decline of the Apache religion and its practices. It is vital to the survival of the religion that its followers and believers understand the Apache language because some religious concepts can only be transmitted in it. Many ceremonies, sacred stories, and even ritual instructions are to be told in the Apache tongue, and this cannot be done when the children do not speak or understand their language.

Fortunately, due to the Apache men and women who were brave, and perhaps stubborn, in defying the dictates of the schools and churches, enough of the language has survived.

LANGUAGE REVITALIZATION EFFORTS TODAY

Several of the Apache languages, like the Jicarilla Apache, the Lipan, and Chiricahua of Fort Sill, are on the endangered list. This means that within the next several decades they may become extinct. Since the late 1960s, concerted efforts have been made to save and preserve the Apache languages. Today, the Apache tribes have created language dictionaries, collected stories and published them, brought the language into their public schools, and established their own ways to preserve and encourage the speaking of their languages.

TRADITIONAL AND MODERN APACHE ART

Art is very much a part of Apache culture. The traditional art of the Apache consists of decorations found on household tools and utensils, including pottery and baskets; on weapons like bows and arrows; on musical instruments; on ceremonial items like sculpted masks; and on costumes worn by ceremonial dancers, and ceremonial dress worn by all ages at different religious events. This traditional art has served as the basis for modern Apache art.

In the past, traditional arts and crafts were made from materials found in nature, like wood of various types for the manufacture of bows and arrows; different animals skins for ceremonial dress; sumac, willow, and yucca and dyes from plants for baskets. It is rare today for Apaches to use all natural materials. Tanned buckskin for clothing, bags, drums, moccasins, belts, and hats; rattles, glass beads both of domestic and foreign manufacture, beads made from bone and horn, bells of all sizes, feathers of all varieties, can all be purchased in specialty shops, trading posts, catalogues, vendors, and online.

Traditional crafts like basket weaving, pottery making, and beading, which served primarily utilitarian purposes in the past, have become art in contemporary times. Making pottery and doing beadwork are not skills required to make a living. It is their aesthetic preservation as art that keeps the identity of the Apache culture alive and serves as a way for artists and artisans to express their creativity and make a living. It is now the artist's skill and creativity that mostly determines what is art and what are crafts.

Throughout the past two centuries, primarily Apache women have preserved traditional Apache art. It is the types of crafts, like basket weaving and pottery making, by women that has survived into the modern period. Basket weaving has been a part of all Apache tribal societies. Pottery making has been a practice among the Jicarilla Apache, especially those that lived near the upper Rio Grande watershed of northern New Mexico.[13] Beadwork was adopted wholeheartedly in the mid-1800s when Apaches began trading with other Indian tribes who had access to the European American trade goods. Apache men have long made weapons, ceremonial items, and horse gear, but they have not become the standard of art items like baskets, beadwork, and pottery. In recent times, however, there has been a revival in the arts traditionally made by male members of the tribes.

How one becomes an artist today involves several routes and pathways. Young artists attend art institutes, colleges, or technical schools to learn various forms of art, while others become apprentices to skilled artisans, and still others are just creative people who are self-taught. Many Apache artists are professionals and make a living from selling their art.

TRADITIONAL ART

As hunters and gatherers, Apache people did not collect art per se; however, their art was part of their lifestyle. If for Shakespeare the whole world was a stage, for the Apache the whole world was an art gallery. Nature provided the artistry, the wonder, and the miracle of creation. Nature was the quintessential form of creativity, and there was little need to replicate it or collect it. One only had to appreciate and show gratitude for the beauty of the earth— from the flowers in the field, to the birds in the trees, the stars scattered over the night sky, the floating bubbles down a stream or river, and the gradations of yellow, orange, and purple created by a Southwest sunset.

The art they did create was often symbolic, beautiful, and utilitarian. They decorated their dress and moccasins, cradleboards, ceremonial gear, and their bows and arrows with various types of designs with contrasting materials and different colors. The traditional art of the Apaches showed up primarily on the ceremonial dress and gear and on their regalia for special events.

BASKET WEAVING TODAY

Apache Indian baskets have been recognized throughout the world for their beauty, quality of construction, and unique designs. Using basically two basket-weaving techniques, twining and coiling, Apache artists have created a wide variety of baskets that function as containers and trays. The techniques, from the harvesting of the plant materials to the use of various types of weaving, have been handed down through successive generations of

Types of modern Jicarilla Baskets. (Courtesy of Sam Minkler, Navajo-Diné photographer, Flagstaff, AZ)

women, usually from within an extended family grouping. Basket weaving is still an art form dominated by women. While working within the confines of tribal basketry traditions, the women have woven their own individual artistry into each basket, creating change, innovation, and vitality to the art form through the introduction of new designs, shapes, and materials. Each basket is an identifiable product of a specific Apache tribe as well as a creation of the individual artist.

Contemporary Apache baskets are all handmade using a combination of traditional and modern weaving techniques, materials, and designs. While the baskets of the Western and Eastern Apache groups differ from each other in several distinct ways, they also share numerous characteristics that make them Apache baskets.

Over the generations there has been a noticeable consistency in the way the Apache baskets were made and in the way designs were used. Coiling has been the foundational weaving technique for all Apache artists. The manufacture of coiled bowls and trays in various shapes, sizes, and designs is common. All the Apache baskets share the distinction that they are made from natural materials like willow, sumac, cottonwood, yucca, and Gambel oak. The common types of designs are geometric and animal and human figures. Different weaving techniques add contrasting and textural elements to the basic designs. Using materials like fringed buckskin or suede, tin, and beads can also accentuate the design. Only the Western Apaches use the twining method of weaving for their wide array of burden baskets and water bottles. The Mescalero Apache have introduced the deep cylindrical or oval, vertical-sided boxes with flat bottoms, often with fitted lids.[14]

Historically, the purpose for baskets was utilitarian. Baskets were made primarily for use as household utensils and tools, for carrying objects, storing, and as water containers. Baskets were also for use in religious ceremonies and were not for sale to outsiders. The baskets had a connection to one's family and their legacy. Family groups become known for the use of various designs or the sizes that were made. Oftentimes, these designs were jealously guarded and protected. It was understood that only members of a particular family grouping could use those designs.

Apache baskets have not remained static but have evolved over time. Changing social and economic circumstances have influenced the making of baskets. The placement of Apaches on Indian reservations had the effect of nearly wiping out the traditional way of basket making, but there has been a revival in the recent past. Basket makers responded to Southwestern art market demands. All the tribes changed their baskets, particularly their designs, to appeal to tourists and visitors. With a demand for other kinds of baskets, Jicarilla women began to use different designs, like fishing tackle boxes or creels, clothes hampers with lids and handles, and shapes embellished with pedestals and loop handles.[15]

Two women most responsible for the revival of basketry at San Carlos were Evelyn and Cecilia Henry, who were still making twined baskets in 1986. The majority of the pitched baskets produced at this time were base-shaped rather than bottle-shaped. Coiled basketry has recently shown some signs of revival, although the recovery has been slow. Though new basket makers use innovative designs, the basket techniques and materials are still traditional.[16]

Western Apache Basketry

There are three major types of Western Apache baskets: the coiled tray and plates, the burden basket, and the urn-shaped twined water bottle. The coiled baskets have two basic shapes: wide, shallow bowls and the twined urn of various sizes. The burden baskets are conical-shaped like deep buckets, with slightly round, pointed bottoms and nearly flaring straight sides.

The use of willow is most common in the coiled baskets and in burden baskets. Traditional Western Apache coiled baskets were made with coils of three rods, and sewn with very fine wooden splints. All the designs incorporate the black circle of the rim and the black disk at the center. Some designs are quite simple, while others incorporate a number of motifs to create complex results. The most common designs in coiled bowls radiate from the center to the rim, producing whorls or whirlwinds and converted into zigzag-like turning motifs. The basic motifs are diamonds, triangles, and rectangles. Western Apache basketry decorations are especially noted for the incorporation of crosses and life forms such as dogs, deer, and men and women. The coiled water jars are of a medium size, with lugs or handles and a coating of piñon pitch to hold water. The application of pitch seals both interior and exterior surfaces, which are usually prepared by rubbing red ochre and/or crushed juniper twigs into the coils.[17]

The Western Apaches used twining almost exclusively for the production of burden baskets. Many are constructed on a stiff frame formed by two heavy rods bent into U shapes, which cross at the bottom of the baskets with the fourth straight sections forming the corners. These burden baskets are almost always decorated with encircling bands of color and embellished with vertical strips of colored and fringed suede or buckskin.[18]

One San Carlos basket maker, Evelyn Henry, explains that she uses different kinds of willows, sumac, and cottonwood for her burden baskets. From the natural-colored willows, she gets black, red, maroon, yellow, green, brown, orange, and gray, and from cottonwood, white. Her designs are images of deer, Crown Dancers, butterflies, and zigzag lines that represent the mountains. Tin cones are attached to the ends of the buckskin fringe, something she credits her mother for reintroducing in the 1950s and 1960s.[19]

Twining burden baskets are still produced by the San Carlos Apaches and to a lesser extent by the White Mountain Apaches. These baskets are used mainly for the Sunrise Ceremony to carry the gifts for the girls, but are also sold. Some twine water baskets are similar in shape to the coiled water jars of the other Apaches, with wide, flaring necks, flat or recessed bases, and handles on the shoulders.

Mescalero Apache Basketry

Mescalero Apache coiled baskets are made in three basic shapes: shallow, circular bowls or trays; the deep cylindrical or oval, vertical-sided boxes with flat bottoms, often with fitted lids; and water bottles. The vertical box-shaped baskets average about seven to nine inches and are unique in the Southwest because they are made with thin half-inch to one-inch slats of Gambel oak or willow instead of rods.[20] The sumac lids are either flat or domed and fitted to the basket by vertical wooden flanges around the edges. The popular designs are zigzag lines, diamonds, and crosses. Water bottles, also called *ollas*, are made using the coiled method and pitched inside and out. Some of the water bottles are unpitched and decorated with geometric designs. They come in several shapes but the common ones are globular with flat bottoms and short, flaring, or cylindrical necks. The twined basket is similar to the baskets of the Western Apache.

The coiled baskets are built on two to three sumac rods stacked one on top of the other. On top of the rods is a thin bundle of yucca fibers or bear grass. The flat, rather wide coils are sewn together with strips or splints of yucca leaves, producing a thin flexible basket wall.[21] The colors of the coiled baskets are subtle and delicate. The base color is khaki tan with designs derived from materials used in stitching the coils to get mottled yellow, amber, or yellow ochre and maroon red. The common design elements and motifs are stars with five or more arms, petals, geometric diamonds, triangles, spiral whirlwinds, and sometimes human or animal forms.

Jicarilla Apache Basketry

Contemporary Jicarilla Apache coiled baskets are made from sumac and willow and are of three basic types: the shallow bowls in various sizes from about 10 to 17 inches in diameter, elongated trays of various sizes; cylindrical storage baskets, some with lids; and the occasional water jug basket with a fringe of leather and horsetail handles, and piñon pitch only on the inside. The baskets are decorated with bold geometric designs, except for the water jug, which usually has no woven designs. These baskets are mainly for decorative uses, except special baskets made for the Bear Dance.[22]

Modern basket makers have revived tradition by adding many new colors and by using more traditional designs. Encircling bands of different colors are common, and some bands are made up of small rectangles indented to create triangles and starlike or petal shapes in the center. Complex floral designs and arrangements of triangles and diamonds are fairly common, but life motifs are rare today. Modern baskets are usually smaller and use a three-rod foundation. The splint sewing makes the basket tight and even and the coils hard and solid.

The Jicarilla Apaches, whose tribal name means "little basket makers" in Spanish, became highly skilled weavers and developed a distinctive type of basketry made with five rods with heavy coils and bright decorations. Traditional Jicarilla three-rod coiled bowls and tray baskets were commonly decorated with geometric designs like diamonds, crosses, zigzag bands, and angular animal figures like deer, elk, horses, or dogs. On some baskets the tan or brown vegetal colors were used to blend the figures with the rest of the reddish-brown sumac stitching. Other baskets were decorated with bright aniline, which often faded into the subtle hues. Such designs created a distinctive style of Jicarilla basketry.[23]

In the 1970s, a small group of dedicated women, among them Margarita DeDios, Talchan Piaz Largo, Mattie Quintana, Hazel DeDios, Beloria Tiznado, Columbia Vigil, Mattie Vicenti, Louise Atole, and Tanzanita Pesata, produced a modest renaissance in traditional Jicarilla basketry. With the support of the tribe, these women gathered at the tribal museum and were paid an hourly wage to make baskets. Their products, as well as other Apache artists' work, were marketed through the museum arts and crafts center.

The gathering of the women provided experimentation with natural dyes and various materials. Lydia Pesata is acknowledged as one of the most experienced users of vegetal colors. She produces a soft yellow with a flower, possibly goldenrod; black from boiled piñon gum; soft pink red from moss; black maroon red from chokecherries; deep red from the bark of the mountain mahogany root; greens from bitterroot; and orange or red grounds from alder bark.[24]

Many of the Apache basket makers today have become quite famous for their art and designs. It is not uncommon to see Apache baskets at local fairs, art fairs and festivals, museums and galleries. The basket-making tradition is probably the best-known Apache art. It is the one art form that has survived through today and continues to rise as an art form that is taught at many tribal cultural centers.

BEADWORK

Beadwork is another form of traditional art that has been adopted by all the Apache tribes. It is not certain when the Apaches began beading their clothing and belongings, but it is now considered an Apache art form in part because of its extensive use. In many ways, this art form is more widely practiced because of the affordability and availability of materials. Unlike basket-making supplies, those needed for beading can be inexpensive, more accessible to the average person and easily purchased. Beading does not require natural materials that are rarely available. Beading is used on everything from headbands, necklaces, and bracelets to belts, traditional ceremonial gear, and buckskin outfits. Looms of various sizes are used as well as different kinds and types of beads. Beading can also be done directly onto cloth, suede, buckskin, leather, blankets, etc. Items such as necklaces, purses, earrings, and bracelets can be beaded without a backing.

Initially, beading was used to decorate the cape portion of the puberty dress. This is still true among the Jicarilla Apaches. Later, beading was used on hundreds of articles. White Mountain Apache girls wear T-necklaces during their Sunrise Ceremony at puberty. This necklace is an essential part of their costumes. These necklaces can be associated with the four cardinal directions: yellow for the east, white for the south, blue and green for the west, and black for north.

POTTERY

Pottery is an art usually associated with the Pueblo Indians, but it has been an art among the Jicarilla Apache women for many generations. During the 1860s through the 1880s the Jicarilla women made micaceous pottery that they sold to the New Mexican Hispanic settlements and Rio Grande Pueblos. What was unique about their pottery was that it was made with micaceous clay that withstood high temperatures and did not easily shatter. It was coated with piñon or aspen pitch to make it waterproof. It was noted not only for its resistance to high heat, but for its thin walls, lightweight construction, and its simple design. It was not sold as a decorative item but sold for its utilitarian

One of Apache artist Tammie Allen's sculptures. (Courtesy of Tammie Allen)

value. The pottery created a very popular market for the Jicarilla women. It was in demand in New Mexican kitchens until the U.S. traders who sold iron products moved in and the Jicarillas were placed on their reservation.

The art of pottery among the Jicarilla Apaches was revived in the early 1970s by Felipe Ortega and Lydia Pesata.[25] In 1982, the Jicarilla Apache Community Video Program featured Sarah Petago, the last known Jicarilla Apache woman who was still using the traditional technique to making pottery. Sarah's preparation to ensure good fortune involved self-purification, binding her hair with a scarf, and building a tepee. It was the Jicarilla belief that clay was the women's spirit and flint was the man's spirit, so Sarah avoided all contact with male members of the tribe, so that the pot did not break before it was completed. Sarah inspired the effort to revive the pottery-making tradition among the Jicarilla Apaches.[26]

Today, the art of pottery is not limited to women, and it has had wide appeal among younger artists, both men and women. Two well-known and award-winning potters are Tammie Allen Walking Spirit and Sheldon Nunez-Velarde. The sale of their pottery is strictly for decorative arts. Tammie makes thin, balanced, highly polished, engaging shapes of pottery using strong lines to help her convey her philosophy that life is continual, with a series of positive and negative events. She states that,

> I learn something new from Mother Earth daily and know I will never master the art of making pottery. I am still growing and I realize that learning is evolutionary and never completed. The clay inspires me and teaches me something new every day. I am constantly humbled by the experience and know the fire, the clay, the wind and the water. Life and clay can never be mastered.[27]

Her award-winning work is found in many galleries throughout the Southwest and is exhibited in places like the Denver Museum of Natural History and Arizona State University.

Sheldon obtains his materials from the clay pits near La Madera, New Mexico. Materials used are micaceous clay and slip. His technique is the hand-coiled method, and coils are blended with scrapers to get a smooth surface. Sheldon's designs are made using clay appliqués such as rope designs. He conducts pottery workshops throughout New Mexico. His pottery is on exhibit at several New Mexico and Arizona galleries and museums.[28]

APACHE PAINTING AND PAINTERS

Painting was not an art associated with the Apache people, but it was a traditional art form for the purpose of decorating items as diverse as deerskins to religious costumes, like the headdresses for the Western Apache Crown

Dancers; for body paint for Jicarilla Apache ceremonial relay runners; and often for horse gear, like the headstalls. In contemporary times, painting is an art that has captured the imagination of many Apache artists.

Apache painters range from those that paint for their personal satisfaction to those who sell their paintings at tribal outlets, fairs, festivals, art shows, galleries, and online. Among the well-known artists is Darren Vigil Gray, a modern abstract-expressionist painter, who is a member of the Jicarilla Apache Nation. One critic wrote that Gray's art has a profound bond to nature, his Apache culture, and to the northern New Mexico landscape. His imagery transcends any particular culture, time, or place. Darren explained: "My culture sustains and nurtures me in the most gentle and positive way. Like the deer, I have an absolute faith and reliance on the natural world. Like my ancestors who came before me, I prefer to approach my art with wild abandonment, free-wheeling nature and spontaneous activity."[29] Paintings by Gray are found in private and public collections of the Smithsonian Institution, the Heard Museum in Phoenix, the Denver Art Museum, Gilcrease Art Museum in Tulsa, and the Museum of Mankind in Vienna, Austria.

Another prominent artist is the San Carlos realism painter Lorenzo Cassa. Cassa states that his art is about the beauty of being Native, specifically Apache. He viewed his art as

"Life . . ." in the simplest terms of the spiritual awakening that results with climbing the hills and hearing an elk bugle, watching an eagle soaring through the canyon, walking through a forest, listening to a stream; you know, the connection with nature and being mesmerized with all of creation. One does not tire from being in the presence of the Creator. I believe this is what my forefathers fought and many died for. The deserts that we see so many artists depict them in, is dreadful and I want to change that. But with all due respect and to keep in the framework of a subject is essential to leave off the ideologies and rely on recorded Apache history to paint Apache culture for expression and precision of a rendering.[30]

Like basket makers, Apache painters are inspired and motivated by their cultural past but use modern methods as well as modern themes to express their art.

SCULPTURE

Although Allan Capron Houser, a Chiricahua Apache, began his career as a painter, his iconic international fame was centered on his sculpture. He was one of the most renowned Native American modern sculptors of the twentieth century. Born in Fort Sill on June 30, 1914, as Allan Haozous, he spent his early life on his family's farm on their Indian allotment. In the late 1930s he entered the Santa Fe Indian School and soon found himself as a painter. His work was associated primarily with the U.S. Southwest. His early art graced the halls of the U.S. Department of the Interior in Washington, D.C. He established a reputation as an Indian painter.

It was not until he reached the age of 50 that he began his career as a professional sculptor, attempting to transcend the parochial boundaries of "Indian art." Like many other Apache artists, Houser celebrates his Apache heritage in most of his works. As a great grandson of Mangas Colorado on his mother's side and the grandnephew of Geronimo on his father's side, his art and sculptures depict his tribal history and the legacy of his people. His culture was his inspiration and he portrayed his people's inner strength, character, and beauty; a "way of being and of knowing the world."[31] As W. Jackson Rushing III wrote in his book *Allan Houser*, "What Houser offered his audience was quiet and highly personal cultural politics, in which he addressed racism against American Indians and the historical violent persecution of Native peoples, including members of his own family. He accomplished this by being a self-effacing, but self-respecting "fine artist," whose beautiful objects embodied the pride, honor, and tenacity of Native Americans."[32] His stone, steel, and bronze sculptures have received international acclaim and are in major museums, galleries, and private collections throughout the United States and Europe. There are many Apache sculptors who have been inspired by Houser, and he has been followed by his sons, Bob and Phillip Houser, who are artists and sculptors in their own right.

PRESERVATION OF TRADITIONAL AND MODERN CULTURAL ARTS AND HISTORY

All the Apache tribes have made concerted efforts, especially in the last several decades, to preserve their traditional and modern cultural arts and history. There are cultural centers, museums, galleries, historic sites, and landmarks located on the reservations where various aspects of the tribe's history are featured. Products like books, paintings, sculptures, arts and crafts, baskets, beaded necklaces, belts, and traditional and modern dress made of buckskin and cloth are sold at these places. Local tribal artists make most of the products.

At Camp Verde, the Yavapai-Apache Cultural Center houses the offices of Yavapai and Dil zhéé Apache Cultural Preservation, and offers language programs for both Yavapais and Apaches, provides a traditional basket-weaving class, and displays the tribal art and artifact collections. The cultural programs are overseen by the Yavapai Elders' Cultural Advisory Committee, who define cultural priorities for the tribe and offer counsel to the administration and council regarding heritage and language preservation issues.[33]

Located at the foot of the White Mountains, Old Fort Apache, listed on the National Register of Historic Places, is owned and operated by the White Mountain Apache Tribe. Old Fort Apache is recognized for its association with Geronimo and Cochise, famous leaders from the various Apache bands who were pursued by soldiers from Fort Apache. The fort serves as the focal point for the protection, celebration, and revitalization of the tribe's culture and history; it is the only former U.S. military base under the interpretive control of an Indian tribe. The nearby White Mountain Apache Cultural Center (House of Our Footprints) serves as a repository for the tribe's cultural heritage through the preservation of oral histories, archival materials, and objects of cultural, historical, and artistic significance. Using exhibits and educational programs, the center fosters an appreciation for the history and cultural traditions of the White Mountain Apache people. The center developed an artist-in-residence program in 1999 to provide opportunities for local artists to develop their skill and show their work to the public. Other historic sites include the Kinishba archaeological ruins, petroglyph sites, and Geronimo's Cave.[34]

The San Carlos Apache Tribe opened a cultural center in 1995 in Peridot, Arizona. The "Window on Apache Culture" is an exhibit that describes the Apache's spiritual beginnings and ceremonies such as the Changing Woman Ceremony. The center staff offers cultural education and demonstrations for schools and other groups.[35]

The Mescalero Apache Tribe has a cultural center, which not only has exhibits but a gallery. St. Joseph's Church has been restored and a request submitted to the National Park Service to add it to the National Register of Historic Places. The Mahi Ke Daada Haax Art Gallery is also located on the reservation. It features original fine art by Mescalero Apache tribal members.[36]

The Jicarilla Apache Tribe has a cultural center, located within the historic district that is on the State and National Register of Historic Places. The center has an exhibit area; a gift shop that sells traditional dress, beadwork, books, native plants used for medicinal and ceremonial use, and artwork by tribal members; and offices and meeting space. It offers an array of cultural activities and programs including a language program, and provides services and equipment to support traditional events and ceremonies. There are also archaeological sites within the reservation boundaries.

The Fort Sill Apache and Apache Tribes of Oklahoma have tribal museums that display exhibits depicting their history and offer arts and crafts products made by their members. One of the most famous stone sculptures, *The Chiricahua Apache Family*, made by its celebrated native son, Allan Houser, is located in front of the Fort Sill Apache Tribal Office.

MUSIC, SONGS, AND DANCE

Song and Dance

Dancing and singing very often go together, especially in religious ceremonies. The music is the songs accompanied by drumming. The ritual dances have been around for centuries and they remain the same today. There are basically two types of Apache religious ceremonies that require dancing and singing. One type is the ceremony performed for individuals, such as the Jicarilla Apache puberty feast (Keesta), or for small groups, like a family prayer meeting. In these instances, one medicine man can be the sole singer or he can have other people helping him, and the person or persons for whom the ceremony is conducted is required to dance. In the individual ceremony, a person dances alone or with a partner. The dances accompany a specific song or set of songs and are usually to the rhythm of a drumbeat. One person or a whole troupe of men and sometimes women can sing the songs. For religious ceremonies, the repertoire of songs is sacred prayer songs and is sung in a set order. The movement of the stars times some of the songs, as in the Mescalero puberty rites. The steps and body movements can vary with the speeding up or slowing down of the singing and drumming.

The other type of dancing and singing is the tribal religious ceremony, which can be conducted solely as a religious ceremony, or it can be a religious ceremony that also invites social dancing. The religious ceremonies are performed by a select group of men who are accompanied by singers, and they are performed for large tribal groups, like the Mountain Spirit Dance for the Western Apache or Go-Jii-Ya for the Jicarilla Apache relay races. For these ceremonies, at designated times everyone can join in the dancing and the dancing becomes a part of the religious ceremony. There is still another religious ceremony that can include social dancing like at the puberty feasts. The Mescalero Apache, for example, have the back and forth social dancing that takes place on the feast grounds during the day and the round dances in the late evening after the Crown Dancers have completed their dancing.

Religious Ceremonial Dances

In the ceremonial dances, like the Western Apache Gah or Mountain Spirit Dances, and the Jicarilla Apache Bear Dances, the men are the dancers and the singers. The sacred prayers are the songs and go together with the dancing. The songs are prayers requesting the Great Spirit to keep the balance in the universe, to keep the seasons intact, to keep the rains coming, to keep the plant life bountiful, and to keep the people safe, happy, and prosperous. Women are invited to dance at certain times during the ceremonies, but not with the men conducting the ceremonies. The dancing by the women is reserved and gentle.

Social Dance

There are a vast number of Indian social dances. The most popular today are the dances at the tribal pow-wows that Apache people attend on their own reservations, other Indian reservations and communities, and in urban areas. The pow-wows are usually intertribal dances, like the southern straight or fancy dances, for both adult men and young boys starting from the age of four. The Jicarilla Apache have adopted the Plains Indian style of war dancing, so the style of dancing at pow-wows and other gatherings fits into their agenda. The Apache women can also participate at the pow-wows in the dance categories of fancy shawl or southern buckskin or cloth dances.

Modern Dances

Other types of dancing include Western-style dancing, like line dancing. Apache students, especially those in college, are exposed to all forms of modern dancing, from ballroom dancing to hip-hop and all dances associated with the general U.S. public.

Modern Music

In addition to the Apache ceremonial and social songs, there is traditional Native American music that often includes drumming, the shaking of rattles, and other percussion instruments. Individuals also play flutes and whistles generally made of wood or bone.

The most widely practiced public musical form among Native Americans in the United States is that of the pow-wow. At pow-wows, drum groups consisting of anywhere from six to ten singers or more sit in a circle around a large drum and play in unison while they sing songs generally written in a Native language. They provide the pow-wow dancers with the music and songs. Popular pow-wow songs include honor songs, flag songs, intertribal songs, sneak-up songs, grass-dances, two-steps, going-home songs, war songs, and even family songs.[37] There are numerous local Apache singer groups on all the Apache reservations that provide songs and music for the tribal celebrations, events, and pow-wows.

Performers of Native American parentage have occasionally appeared in the U.S. popular music scene, including Apaches like Darren Vigil Gray, who is also a famous impressionist painter, and who has a rock and roll band in Santa Fe. A. Paul Ortega, a member of the Mescalero Apache Tribe, is credited with creating a sound that forever revolutionized the landscape of Native American music. He came into the limelight in the early 1960s, when he began using and combining Apache songs with the guitar, bass drum, and harmonica. His first albums, *Two Worlds* and *Three Worlds*, draw upon Native culture storytelling and vocals that come from the soul of the Apache. These albums became modern classics of contemporary Native American music.[38] Apache musicians have followed in his footsteps; many have branched out into other U.S. musical genres.

TRADITIONAL DRESS

Modern-day Apache traditional dress is worn only on two occasions, one for the puberty ceremonies for the girls and religious ceremonial dress for the men, and the other for celebratory tribal events and occasions. Both types of modern traditional dress have their origin from, and are patterned on, the traditional dress worn for religious ceremonies. The styles for the ceremonial dress have remained basically the same since the period of contact. The difference from then and now is the way the entire costume is made, the materials used, and the decorations and accessories. The modern traditional dress for celebrations and official tribal events is made from cloth material and is an adaptation of the Western pioneer man and woman's dress, and with stylized touches from the traditional Apache dress.

Traditional Dress for Religious Ceremonies

There are both distinct differences and similarities between the religious ceremonial dress of the Western and Eastern Apache women. Both ceremonial dresses are two pieces consisting of a fringed cape worn over a gown-style dress with fringes made from buckskin. The young girls wear these dresses during the Sunrise Ceremony for the Western Apaches and the puberty feast for the Jicarilla Apaches. Often there is a combination cloth and buckskin version of the ceremonial dress. Moccasins are knee-length for the Jicarillas, and the short top for the Western Apaches. Accessories include the T-beaded necklace for the Western Apaches and the choker made of bone beads and earrings of round abalone shells with two magpie feathers tied to the back of the hair. The girl can wear as many rings and bracelets as she wishes and most of them are silver jewelry with turquoise, red or black coral, or blue lapis stones. A plain buckskin cape with the tail of the deer still attached is also worn over the dress and cape. The order of dress is symbolic and must be followed. Prayers are sung as the girl puts on the dress, then the cape, shoes and leggings, belt, necklace, earrings, bracelet, and rings.

Christina Harrison (Jicarilla Apache), in her Keesta dress made by her grandmother, Rebecca Martinez. (Courtesy of Lucien Niemeyer)

The outside cape is draped over the dress, then the face is painted, and a straw is provided as a scratch stick. The young boy is also dressed while the songs are being sung, beginning with the breechcloth, shirt (shirt is not required), beaded vest, followed by the leggings, a bone-bead necklace that looks like a breastplate, and lastly hoop earrings.[39]

Modern Traditional Dress for Tribal Events and Occasions

The modern traditional dress for girls and women for tribal events and occasions is the two-piece blouse and skirt or the ankle-length dress with a

San Carlos woman wearing a combination cloth and buckskin dress for sunrise ceremony. (Courtesy of Sheldon Nunez-Velarde. Jicarilla Apache)

wide cape-like piece of cloth sewn to the shoulder that hangs over the sleeves. These dresses are made with wide variety of colorful print or plain cloth from silk to polyester to cotton.

The Western Apache style is a two-piece dress with a blouse with a squared or V-neckline, three-fourths or full-length puffy sleeves, that hangs over the skirt down to the hips. The bottom is a wide gathered skirt that is tiered by two to three pieces of cloth, or it can be one color with rickrack or bias tape. The standard length is down to the middle of the calves. This combination of types of materials, print or plain, and the colors are endless, and are limited only by the creativity of the maker. Worn with this dress are strings of beads, the T-beaded necklace, or other types of necklaces and earrings of every imaginable style. The hairstyle of the girls and women is usually straight and long with small buckskin ties to hold feathers or other accessories. Many girls and women have short hair and that is acceptable. Moccasins are worn with the dress and they are made of buckskin with or without fringes. A burden basket can be strapped onto the back or a beaded fringed buckskin purse can finish off the outfit.

The Jicarilla Apache dress for girls and women for modern tribal events and activities consists of a one-piece dress with a V-neck or rounded neckline that is ankle length with a cape type sleeve. Colorful silk ribbons can be sewn around the front and back of the shoulder piece. A wide black leather belt at least three to five inches wide with two or three buckles is worn with the dress. The belt is adorned around the top and bottom edges with silver studs or bronze conchos. This leather belt can also be beaded. The moccasins are either plain or beaded and are either the knee- or ankle-length type. The knee-length usually has fringes and it can also be beaded in its entirety or beaded on the top and along the edges. The jewelry consists of hoop earrings and a choker. The earrings are made from round abalone shell with coral or glass beads. A two- or three-stranded necklace choker is made from white bone beads attached with cotton or leather string and tied in the back. This dress is worn with a fringed shawl made with all types of cloth material. The shawl can be plain, of one color, or it can be decorated with ribbons, glitter, and beads. Many of the Apache royalty can also have their tribal logos attached to the back, or they can have their titles on the shawls.

Mescalero Apache Crown Dancers' Dress

The dress of the Mountain Spirit Dancers (also called Crown Dancers or Gah Dancers) is inspired by and represents the sacredness of the ceremony. Although the dances were traditionally only performed for Apache people, today these dancers perform publicly and widely throughout the United States at various events. All Western Apache tribal dancers perform them. The dress style and material varies from tribe to tribe but they all have standard components, consisting of the signature headdress from which comes the name Crown Dancers; the dark mask; the bandana; armband; sash; belt; turned-up toed buckskin moccasins; and fringed kilt or skirt.

The entire dress is symbolic of the four directions. The designs on the headdress, the sticks carried by the Crown Dancers, the upper torso painted in black, and the designs painted on the front and back upper torso of the dancers can be of different designs but must represent the sacred. The sword-like sticks are painted with four designs repeated in units of four, with four colors to represent the four directions. These designs match the headdresses, which are attached to the top of the mask and have turkey feathers. The dancers wear heavy skirts about their waists that may be made of canvas but mostly of buckskin. These skirts have from one to three pieces that have the appearance of being horizontally layered and the sides and bottom are fringed and usually have attached metal cone jingles. The skirts are held up with wide belts decorated with metal designs that coordinate with the rest of the dress design. A red sash is tied in the back around the waist and it falls down over the rear of the skirt.[40] The symbolic dress is given special care, with prayers made at all stages, from the time the materials are gathered to the time they are put on and taken off to the time they are returned to the earth when they are worn out.

The language, art, music, song and dance, and the traditional dress of the Apache people have many common characteristics that tie their past to the present. These cultural arts find their foundations in their reverence for their physical environment, their lands, and their people, even if the art is a modern American art or the Apache person makes his or her home away from the reservation. The survival of the language and the arts reflect that there is a pride in being Apache. The commonalities among the Apache artists are surprising considering the physical distances between them in contemporary times. The Apache tribal language and arts and culture have entered a new phase of renewal and revival. The trend for the future will see even more promotion of arts by the tribes, and an increase in the number of artists and the number of Apache speakers.

Notes

1. Robert W. Young, "Apachean Languages," in *Southwest*, vol. 10 of *Handbook of North American Indians*, volume ed. Alfonso Ortiz (Washington: Smithsonian Institution Press, 1983), 393–400.

2. Mescalero Apache Cultural Center Director, Telephone Conversation with Author, March 2010.

3. White Mountain Apache Cultural Director, Telephone Conversation with Author, March 2010.

4. San Carlos Apache Cultural Director, Telephone Conversation with Author, March 2010.

5. American Indian Statistics by Social and Economic Factors (2000 Census), "Percentage of non-English Language Use in AIAN Areas Persons 5 and older," http://www.ovc.edu/missions/indians/indsocia.htm (accessed March 30, 2010).

6. Conversation with Michael Darrow, Fort Sill Apache Tribe, March 2010.

7. Apache Tribe of Oklahoma Administrator, Telephone Conversation with Author, March 2010.

8. Phone, Wilhelmina, Maureen Olson, and Matilda Martinez, *Dictionary of Jicarilla Apache* (Albuquerque: University of New Mexico Press, 2007), 58.

9. Ibid.

10. Martin W. Ball, "Mountain Spirits: Embodying the Sacred in Mescalero Apache Tradition," Ph.D. diss., University of California, Santa Barbara (Ann Arbor: UMI Dissertation Services: 2000), 41–43.

11. Claire R. Farrer, *Living Life's Circle: Mescalero Apache Cosmovision* (Albuquerque: University of New Mexico Press, 1991), 28.

12. Williamson, Ray A., *Living the Sky: The Cosmos of the American Indian* (Norman: University of Oklahoma Press, 1987), 30.

13. Veronica E. Tiller, *The Jicarilla Apache Tribe: A History* (Albuquerque: BowArrow Publishing Company, 1983), 57.

14. Whiteford, Andrew Hunter, "The Apaches," *Southwestern Indian Baskets: Their History and Their Makers* (Santa Fe: School of American Research Press, 1989), 45–92.

15. Ibid., 50.

16. Ibid., 88–90.

17. Ibid., 90.

18. Ibid., 87.

19. "Evalena Henry," http://www.sancarlosapache.com/Evalena_Henry.htm (accessed January 14, 2010).

20. Whiteford, *Southwestern Indian Baskets*, 58.

21. Ibid., 56.

22. Lydia Pesata, et al., *Jicarilla Basket Making*, A Project of Native Arts and Crafts Cultural Awareness Program, ESAA (Loveland, Colo.: Center for In-Service Education, 1975), 15–30.

23. Whiteford, *Southwestern Indian Baskets*, 50.

24. Ibid., 51.

25. Interviews with Tammie Allen and Sheldon Nunez-Velarde, April 12, 2010.

26. Jicarilla Apache Community Education Video Program, *Jicarilla Apache Pottery* (Dulce: Jicarilla Apache Tribe, 1982), 4.

27. Tammie Allen, E-mail to Author, April 23, 2010.

28. Sheldon Nunez-Velarde, E-mail to Author, April 14, 2010.

29. Lew Allen Galleries, "Darren Vigil Gray Bio," http://www.lewallengalleries.com (accessed January 12, 2010).

30. "Artist Statement," http://www.lorenzoCassa.com (accessed January 14, 2010).

31. Rushing III, W. Jackson, *Allan Houser, An American Master (Chiricahua Apache, 1914–1994)* (New York: Harry N. Abrams, Inc., Publishers, 2004), 225.

32. Ibid., 11.

33. Tiller, Veronica E. Tiller, Compiler, *Tiller's Guide to Indian Country: Economic Profiles of American Indian Reservations* (Albuquerque: BowArrow Publishing, 2005), 291.

34. Ibid., 300.

35. San Carlos Apache Cultural Center, http://www.sancarlosapache.com/San _Carlos_Culture_Center.htm (accessed January 15, 2010).

36. *Tiller's Guide*, 737.

37. American Indian dances, http://www.answers.com/topic/american-indian (accessed March 3, 2010).

38. Native American Music Since 1951, Canyon Records, http://www.store.canyonrecords.com/index.php?app=ccp0&ns=prodshow&ref=CR-7077 (Accessed March 10, 2010).

39. Roberta E. Serafin, Conversation with Author, April 10, 2010.

40. Ball, "Mountain Spirits," 174–175.

4

Modern Lifestyle, Housing, Employment, and Education

THE MODERN APACHE LIFESTYLE is directly related to the rural location of their reservations in the southwestern states of Arizona, New Mexico, and Oklahoma and to their historical and legal relationship with the U.S. federal government. It has been defined by modernization in only the last couple of decades. Prior to that time, the way that the Apache lived was marred with poverty and its economic and social consequences. Through the changes in federal Indian policies in recent decades and the commercialization of Indian gaming, Apache people finally have a lifestyle of modernity, with decent housing, employment, and educational opportunities.

MODERN LIFESTYLE

Modern Apache lifestyle is characterized by the physical locations of their reservations in rural areas within short distances from small non-Indian towns and communities. According to the U.S. Census 2000, the Fort Apache and San Carlos Apache Reservations were ranked in the top 25 most populous Indian Reservations in the United States, with Fort Apache at 11,854 and San Carlos at 9,065.[1] The Jicarilla Reservation had a population of 2,755, and the Mescalero had 3,156.[2] There were no exact population figures for the Oklahoma Apache Tribes because their numbers were figured into the population for the entire census tract in their areas that included non-Indians.

Nationally, in 2000, out of a total of 4.3 million American Indians, there were 57,199 Apache Indians who reported only one American Indian tribal group to which they belonged. This group made up .02 percent of the entire U.S. population. There were 104,556 Apache Indians who reported one American Indian tribal group in combination with one or more races. This group made up .04 percent of the entire U.S. population. The median age of all Apaches was 29 years. The under-18-year-old group made up 33.5 percent of the Apache population, and the 18-to-64-year-old group made up the largest group at 61.9 percent, followed by the over-65-year old at 4.4 percent.[3] In 2004, the national population for Apaches who were only Apache by blood was reported at 66,048.[4]

Like average Americans who live in a rural area, most Apache people live in modern homes with all modern conveniences, their children attend public schools, and they obtain their wages and income by working 40 hours per week for their employers, who are primarily governmental entities. They listen to the same radio programs and watch the same television networks and cable programs, and have access to all the consumer products, from automobiles to candy bars. Their rural locations define the types of housing they live in, the access they have to acquiring modern conveniences, their choices for recreation and entertainment, employment and educational opportunities open to them, and the kinds of community facilities and services available to them.

The differences between the Apache tribal communities and their non-Indian neighbors are many; some are invisible, or not well known, and often not understood by either the dominant U.S. society at large or their close non-Indian neighbors. The main differences are ethnically and historically based. The obvious differences are that the majority of people on the Indian reservations are Apache Indians; that the Apache language is spoken; that the native religion is still practiced; and that the native culture and customs are still alive and well, despite assimilation and eradication efforts.

The not-so-obvious differences between the communities stem from Native people's legal relationship with the U.S. federal government, which has determined, and continues to determine through policies and laws, the quality of life on Indian reservations. The federal government, through its historical agreements and as the trustee for the Apache tribes, is responsible for the management of their natural resources, for the education of the Apache people, and for the overall general welfare of the Apache people. Because the federal government has a special trusteeship relationship with the Apache tribes, the status of their reservation lands are inalienable and the lands cannot be sold, mortgaged, or used as collateral for obtaining housing or commercial loans for economic development, unless specifically accounted for in federal legislation. The Apache tribes, and most Native tribes, have been limited in their ability to develop their own economies by the legal restrictions manifested in the relationship with the federal government.

Due to this dependent relationship, the Apache people have historically been poverty-stricken, lacked adequate housing and medical care, received an inadequate education, and have been economically dependent. As a result, the Apache tribes have been either at the bottom of or the top of all social statistics (depending which level is considered the worse), like having the lowest income and educational levels, and the highest rate of school dropouts, highest rates of suicide, high rates of alcohol and drug abuse, and highest rates of unemployment.

Since the development of the U.S. War on Poverty programs under former president Lyndon B. Johnson and the Indian self-determination policies of the 1970s, the government has provided more funding for the improvement of reservation living standards, including the building of community centers, medical clinics, school facilities, housing, and expansion of recreation. However, there continues to be a shortage of federal funding and technical assistance in providing adequate housing, medical care, and economic development on the Apache reservations.

Since the commercialization of Indian gaming in the late 1980s, Apache tribes have finally had surplus revenues for economic development, community infrastructure improvement, and offering community services that are taken for granted in many non-Indian communities. These changes have created more employment and income for families that has led to an improvement in the standard of living. Although this growth is still in the "catch-up phase" in comparison with all other modern rural communities, there are noticeable growth indicators in various economic and social sectors. The economic poverty rate has decreased but has not reached the levels of the rest of the country.

Modern Apache Community Centers and Facilities

Today, the modern lifestyle on the Apache Reservations consists of Apache people having access to all types of community facilities, like community centers, senior citizen centers, teen centers, libraries, computer labs, and health and fitness centers. All Apache tribes have community centers, although some are more elaborate than others and each offer different kinds of facilities, services, and activities.[5]

A new community center on the Yavapai-Apache Reservation at Camp Verde, Arizona, boasts a weight room and gymnasium with hardwood floors. There is a public library, a heritage park that features lighted baseball fields, basketball courts, volleyball courts, and a snack bar. Boys and Girls Clubs meet at the newly constructed Teen Center, which opened in January 2004. The center has computers available for use by young people. There are also summer bowling leagues for the tribal youth. A senior center exists in Clarkdale.

The Tonto Apache community center in Payson, Arizona, consists of a recreation center that has a swimming pool, library, computer room, and youth activity center. In 2003, the tribal offices moved into a new two-story tribal governmental complex with a daycare center. There are three community centers on the Fort Apache Reservation, a rodeo and fairgrounds, an indoor swimming pool, a cultural center, a library, and three gymnasiums. The San Carlos Apache Tribe community facilities include a library, a rodeo arena, and six ball fields.

In New Mexico, the Jicarilla Apache Reservation has a multipurpose community center with a bowling alley, a swimming pool, and a gymnasium. There is a senior citizen center with dining facilities, meeting space, and an office. There is also a cultural center, a library, and a health and fitness center. The recreational facilities include a rodeo arena with camping facilities, a lighted baseball field, and a park. Many recreational facilities are shared with the local public school, such as the football and field track stadium. The Mescalero Apache maintain a community center complete with a swimming pool, gymnasium, library, and bowling alley. There is also a tribal museum, an elderly care center, and a myriad of recreational facilities, including a golf course.

In Oklahoma, the Apache Tribe has a tribal administrative complex that includes offices, meeting facilities, and a museum. At Fort Sill, the Apache Tribe has a community center within its tribal headquarters and it also has a gym, an elders' nutrition program, and an emergency youth shelter.

Law Enforcement and Public Safety

As part of the governmental services offered through tribal governments, law enforcement departments are found on all the Apache reservations to preserve law and order, enforce tribal ordinances, and to cooperate with state and federal law enforcement when they need assistance on tribal lands. Tribal police departments have jurisdiction only on tribal lands, unless they have agreements with the state. Tribal police are in charge of safety during public events, and may arrest people who disturb the peace, who commit domestic violence, or who commit crimes against people or property, among other minor crimes. Anything that is a felony in the state is a felony under federal law under the Assimilative Crimes Act of 1948 and becomes a federal matter. All tribes have juvenile and adult detention facilities and tribal court systems. Fire protection is also afforded to all communities.

Telephone, television and cable, radio, and high-speed Internet services are available on all Apache Reservation lands from regional public service utility companies. Cell phone towers allow all Apache people to have cell phones.

On the San Carlos Reservation, the tribally owned and operated San Carlos Apache Telecommunications Utility provides these services. The reservation receives numerous radio stations from Globe, Safford, Tucson, and Phoenix. Apache Cablevision, owned by the San Carlos Telecommunications Utility, offers basic cable television service to the San Carlos and Peridot areas. The Mescalero Apaches also own Mescalero Apache Telecom, which provides telephone, Internet, and broadband services to reservation customers.

Media and communications services are available on all reservations. Television and radio coverage from national, regional, and local stations are found on all Apache reservations. Many of the Apache tribes publish their own newspapers, and one radio station, KCIE 90.5, has been owned and operated by the Jicarilla Apache since the early 1980s. The *Jicarilla Chieftain* is the tribe's official newspaper. A monthly newspaper, *The Apache Scout*, is published on the Mescalero Apache Reservation and on the Fort Apache Reservation. The *Fort Sill Apache News* is a newsletter published once a month.

Health Care

The modern lifestyle on Apache reservations means having the benefit of medical care. Health care services are provided to the Indian people by the U.S. Indian Health Service (IHS), an agency of the U.S. Public Health Service in the U.S. Department of Health and Human Services. The U.S. Congress funds the IHS each year through appropriation. The IHS reported in 2006 three major facts on Indian health disparities that apply to and include the Apache tribes:

[1] The American Indian and Alaska Native people have long experienced lower health status when compared with other Americans. Lower life expectancy and the disproportionate disease burden exist perhaps because of inadequate education, disproportionate poverty, discrimination in the delivery of health services, and cultural differences. These are broad quality of life issues rooted in economic adversity and poor social conditions.

[2] American Indians and Alaska Natives born today have a life expectancy that is 2.4 years less than the U.S. all races population (74.5 years to 76.9 years, respectively; 1999–2001 rates), and American Indian and Alaska Native infants die at a rate of 8.5 per every 1,000 live births, as compared to 6.8 per 1,000 for the U.S all races population (2000–2002 rates).

[3] American Indians and Alaska Natives die at higher rates than other Americans from tuberculosis (600% higher), alcoholism (510% higher), motor vehicle crashes (229% higher), diabetes (189% higher), unintentional injuries (152% higher), homicide (61% higher) and suicide (62% higher).[6]

With this type of health disparity data and information, the IHS and the federal government have made better efforts to deliver health care to Indian reservations. In the recent past, clinics and hospitals have been built on all the Apache reservations. For services like heart surgery, the Indian Health Service has contracted arrangements with hospitals and doctors in the nearest large cities, like Albuquerque, Santa Fe, Phoenix, and Tucson. IHS provides primary, dental, and inpatient care, and an array of medical programs for behavioral health, cardiology, pediatrics, diabetes, maternal/child health, optometry, and substance abuse.

There is a private hospital in Cottonwood, Arizona, and a U.S. Public Health Service hospital in Camp Verde, Arizona. Public-health nursing services are provided through a contract arrangement with the Yavapai County Health Department. Three community health representatives are employed by the tribe and act as liaisons with the Public Health Service staff. Contract hospital and medical services are authorized through local physicians and clinics in Camp Verde, Clarkdale, Cottonwood, Prescott, and Sedona. Alcohol and substance abuse services and programs in behavioral health are available, as well as nutrition classes and dental care. The Inter Tribal Council of Arizona operates a women's, infants' and children's nutrition program at the food bank in Middle Verde.[7]

New Jicarilla Apache Hospital in Dulce, New Mexico. (Courtesy of Tiller Research Inc. Photo by Everett Serafin)

For the Tonto Apaches, contracted medical services are available at the Payson Regional Medical Center, but the tribe has a Community Health Representative unit for the community. In addition to the government health services that the Tonto Apaches are eligible for, the tribe has a self-funded medical coverage plan for its members and employees.

The larger Apache reservations at Fort Apache and San Carlos have their own medical centers. The Indian Health Service operates a 50-bed hospital at Whiteriver, Arizona, providing a full range of inpatient, outpatient, and community health care. Emergency air evacuations to larger facilities in Phoenix are available by contracted helicopter service. There are various mental health and substance abuse treatment options available on the reservation, and there is an outpatient and emergency care clinic in Cibecue, as well as an EMS unit. On the San Carlos Reservation, there is a 32-bed U.S. Public Health Service hospital, with seven doctors and two staff dentists. The facility includes an emergency room, a laboratory, X-ray services, social and psychological services, and inpatient and outpatient care. There is also a health center at Bylas.

Celebrations, Pow-wows, and Festivals

A vast array of entertainment venues exist on all Apache reservations, from tribal ceremonies to rodeo and annual fair days, festivals, sporting events, entertainment offered by the local casinos, and school-sponsored events. Apache families also travel to statewide and out-of-state towns, cities, and other Indian reservations for pow-wows, rodeos, fairs, and all types of entertainment, recreation, and sports events. The tribal ceremonies, although religious in nature and purpose, are also a source of family gatherings and community dancing. At these ceremonies it is not uncommon to see vendors selling jewelry, arts and crafts, trinkets, souvenirs, toys, blankets, or any other product, similar to what is found at local fairs. These gatherings and events are open to anyone.

Special tribal events on the Fort Apache Reservation attract many locals as well as tourists. In April, there is the Canyon Day Open Show, and in May, there is the Junior Rodeo and the Headstart Rodeo and Parade. The Sunrise Dance Ceremonies begin in May and continue throughout September each year. The Old Timers Junior Rodeo is held in August, followed by the Tribal Fair and Rodeo in September. Mountain Frontier Days, the White Mountain Native American Arts and Crafts Festival, the annual Bluegrass Festival, and the Fall Festival also take place.

On many summer weekends at San Carlos, traditional Apache ceremonies take place, and visitors are allowed to observe portions of some rituals. The casino sponsors a pow-wow each year in February, and in March the tribe

Ashley L. Julian carrying an Edward Curtis photo in comparison with the old and new. (Courtesy of Sheldon Nunez-Velarde, Jicarilla Apache)

holds an Indian Festival. In April, the Mt. Turnbull Rodeo continues a decades-long tradition, and on June 18, the San Carlos Apaches celebrate their Independence Day. The annual All-Indian Rodeo and Fair is held in November.

A number of the Jicarilla Apaches' annual celebrations are open to the public, including the Little Beaver Round-Up held the third weekend in July. It includes the Pro-Indian Open Rodeo, Pony Express Race, 5K Run/Walk, a pow-wow, a parade, traditional dances, and a carnival. The Jicarillas celebrate Go-Jii-Ya Feast, an annual harvest festival, on September 14–15. Activities at this event include ceremonial relay races, a rodeo, and traditional dances. The tribe also hosts the Jicarilla Day Pow-wow the week of February 11, the date of the establishment of the reservation in 1887.

The Mescalero Apaches host the Mescalero Apache Ceremonial and Rodeo in July of each year. Festivities include four days and nights of dancing, eating, and paying tribute to young maidens undergoing tribal puberty rites. In cooperation with the state, the tribe co-hosts the annual Mescal Roast and Celebration at the Living Desert State Park outside Carlsbad, New Mexico.

White Mountain Spirit Dancers performing at Pueblo Cultural Center in Albuquerque. (Courtesy of Dina Velarde)

Indian Royalty and Indian Princesses

A recent phenomenon has been the rise of Indian pageants among all Indian tribes, including the Apache tribes. These royalty pageants are a direct expression of the pride the young girls have in being Apache. Young girls between the ages of about 14 and 21 compete for the title of Miss White Mountain Apache, Miss San Carlos Apache, Miss Jicarilla Apache, etc. These contests are not conducted like the other national and state beauty pageants, where bathing suits and evening gowns are the norm. In the Indian pageants, the young girls wear their traditional regalia and demonstrate their knowledge of their tribal histories and culture, and perhaps a traditional skill like basket weaving or beadwork. These young girls represent the tribes at official events both on and off the reservations. When appearing in official events they wear their tribal traditional dress, their beaded crowns and title sashes. They reign for one year before another girl is selected. In addition, there is usually a court of Indian princesses that accompanies the Miss Apache Tribe. Many of these princesses are younger girls from 8 to 12 years of age. Often these princesses have their own titles independent of the Miss Apache Tribe. Any event can have its own princess and royalty, like a special pow-wow or tribal celebration.

Indian Rodeos

A popular and favorite form of sport entertainment on Apache Indian reservations is rodeo. This sport celebrates the U.S. Western tradition of riding, roping, and bronc-riding; a tradition that included Native Americans, first as part of the exhibitory ambiance reminiscent of the Old West of "cowboys and Indians," then later as participants, contestants, and spectators. It is popular with the Apache people, who have always had a love for horses and who come from cattle ranches and working with livestock. Rodeo has attracted Apache people since it became a sport in the 1930s. The growth of the sport of rodeo has mushroomed since that time.

Indian cowboys and cowgirls compete in the rodeo events that include bareback bronc riding, saddle bronc riding, calf and steer roping, steer wrestling, and barrel racing. On many of the Indian reservations whole families have competed in the sport of rodeo for over half a century, and certain families have been associated with rodeos for many generations. The communities usually sponsor rodeo events, perhaps in conjunction with the tribes. Participants travel throughout the region, state, nation, and even across the globe to compete in the rodeo events, for which they pay an entry fee, and the winners obtain prize money, saddles, trophy buckles, and horse trailers. Rodeo is considered a family event and it is not uncommon to see the father and sons as well as the mother and daughters compete in the rodeo events. Many young men and women devote their entire lives to rodeo and many make a living from their winnings in rodeo competitions, training and selling horses, furnishing roping steers, bucking horses, bulls, and calves. Roping and barrel racing horses are purchased at great expense, along with horse trailers, trucks, and horse gear, as well as the cost of rodeo attire. Young girls and young women also have the opportunity to compete for rodeo royalty consisting of the rodeo queen and her attendants; this also takes time and money. It takes a lot of income to be in the sport of rodeo.

Apache cowboys and cowgirls are very proud to be a part of this Western rural family sport and tradition. It is an industry that every Apache tribal government has supported through the building of rodeo arenas complete with horse facilities, lighted grandstands, and vendor and camping areas. Rodeo events of all types are offered almost year-around on all the Apache reservations, some as special and standalone events or in conjunction with other celebrations, like pow-wows, fairs, or tribal anniversaries.

Sports

Other popular entertainment venues are basketball, football, baseball, and track and field sports. Most of these sports are affiliated with high school teams, for both girls and boys. The high school teams compete throughout the state,

The Apache owned and operated Sunrise ski mountain and resort employs many tribal members bringing jobs to the White River Indian community in Arizona. (Copyright © Marilyn Angel Wynn/Nativestock.com)

including the popular state championship tournaments. Although many communities have community basketball teams and tournaments, the sport remains primarily school-related events. Events such as tennis, gymnastics, swimming, soccer, golf, and skiing have not had wide appeal on reservations. Two of the best ski areas on the White Mountain Apache Reservation in Arizona and the Ski Apache on the Mescalero Apache Reservation have not enticed large numbers of Apaches to the sport of skiing, primarily because of the cost.

Dances and Other Entertainment

There are also other forms of entertainment on Indian reservations, like social dancing at tribal pow-wows, rodeo dances, and school dances. On many Indian reservations there are harvest festivals, arts and crafts shows and festivals, carnivals, bicycle races, motorcycle races, and walking and running races.

Outdoor Sports and Recreation

The Apache tribes have access to a huge array of outdoor activities, like fishing, canoeing, boating, water skiing, trail riding, hiking, mountain climbing, picnicking, and hunting. While most of these outdoor recreational opportunities are directed toward the tourists, they are also open to tribal members, often at discounted rates. Fishing, picnicking, and hunting are by far the most popular of the outdoor activities. In the last decade, with the advent of Indian gaming, golf courses have been built close to tribal casinos; however, the clientele is largely non-Indians.

On the Fort Apache Indian Reservation, the opportunities for outdoor recreation are vast. White Mountain Apache Tribe Wildlife and Outdoor Division activities include a hunting program, a rent-a-lake program, river running, and canyoneering. Fishing, hunting, backcountry safaris and tours, and other outdoor adventures are a huge draw for tourists. Hawley Lake Cabins and Resort is available in McNary, Arizona, within walking distance of Hawley Lake and Earl Park Lake. Because the area is so rich in natural resources, there are innumerable wildlife viewing opportunities along 500 miles of cold streams and 30 artificial lakes, which offer year-round trout fishing and winter ice fishing, as well as a number of tribally operated campgrounds.

HOUSING

Housing on Apache Indian reservations is provided through federal government-funded housing programs. Up through the 1990s, compared to the general U.S. population, the Indian housing was very poor on all Indian reservations; they were overcrowded, and many houses did not have electricity, plumbing, running water, or adequate kitchen facilities. Between 1990 and 2000, the proportion of overcrowded homes on the Apache reservations declined from three and a half times to two and a half times the national rate.

According to the Bureau of the Census, homes built between 1985 and 1990 on reservations were considered new. Among the larger reservations (those with 500 or more American Indian households) such as the Fort Apache Reservation, 25.8 percent lived in new homes (1985 or later), 4.8 percent were still living in homes built prior to 1940, and 87.5 percent of these homes were one-family homes. Living in mobile homes and trailers were 5.5 percent of the population. On the San Carlos Reservation, 28.5 percent of the residents lived in new homes, and 5.6 percent lived in homes built prior to 1940. Of the homes, 89.5 percent were single-family residences and 7.3 percent of the population lived in mobile and trailer houses.[8]

According to the 2000 U.S. Census, 44.1 percent of all Apache households were married couples, 21.3 percent were female households with no spouse present, 7.6 percent were male households with no spouse present, and 27.0 percent were non-family households.[9] The average household consisted of 3.25 people. For the New Mexico Apache tribes, in 2000 there were 972 housing units on the Jicarilla Apache Reservation and 916 on the Mescalero Apache Reservation.[10]

Chart 4.1

Arizona and New Mexico Apache Tribes—1990

	% Living in New Homes	% Living in Old (Pre-1940) Homes	% Living in One-Family Houses	% Living in Mobile/Trailers
Fort Apache	25.8	4.8	87.5	5.5
San Carlos	28.5	5.6	89.5	7.3
Jicarilla Apache	22.9	5.9	75.1	14.2
Mescalero Apache	16.2	18.1	94.5	4.0

Source: U.S. Bureau of the Census, Statistical Brief, Housing of American Indians on Reservations—Structural Characteristics, 1990.

The increase in the number of housing units since 2000 is due to the federal government funding programs in partnership with the Apache tribes; together through their combined and creative efforts they have made a difference in providing housing to Apache people. The Native American Housing Assistance and Self-Determination Act of 1996 (NAHASDA) was signed into law on October 26, 1996 by former president Bill Clinton. NAHASDA was implemented through U.S. Department of Housing and Urban Development (HUD) regulations. It oversees six eligible fundable activities:

- Indian Housing Assistance
- Development
- Housing Services
- Housing Management Services
- Crime Prevention and Safety Activities
- Model Activities[11]

Under this NAHASDA legislation, the White Mountain Apache Housing Authority received a highly competitive grant known as the ROSS grant for its Apache Dawn project. In this highly innovative and model project, the tribe worked out a financial arrangement that involved itself, the state of Arizona, and various federal government agencies that allowed the tribe to issue a tax-exempt bond in the amount of $25 million to initially build 250 new homes and to obtain two loans from the State of Arizona to finance the construction of water and wastewater infrastructure. The number of homes increased to 317 due to savings from construction costs. As a timber-producing tribe, it was able to use materials manufactured at the tribe's timber company, and it was able to utilize tribal employees in the construction of the homes. For the first time, Apache people became homeowners, through assistance offered by the program to qualify for mortgage. This project addressed tribal economic development to sustain tribal communities in having affordable housing. Although the White Mountain Apache Tribe was successful in the development of 317 homes, they are still faced with the funding of housing infrastructure, and these 317 homes constitute only 16 percent of their housing needs. The critical housing shortage remains a top priority for the White Mountain Apache Tribe.[12]

On the Camp Verde Indian Reservation in 2004, the tribe's housing department was involved in rehabilitating 36 low-rent housing units and building new low-income tax credit housing units for tribal members and the community of Middle Verde. This included the addition of twelve duplex units and two laundromats. The tribal housing department built playgrounds near housing units in Clarkdale and Camp Verde. The Yavapai-Apache government's housing priority was not only to provide safe housing but also to do so with an eye toward landscape and the larger ecological environment, so that a sense of tribal community would be fostered.[13]

Another example of a model housing project using a governmental-tribal partnership approach is on the Mescalero Apache Reservation in New Mexico. The first "fully green" housing project, known as *I-Sah'-Din'-Dii*, was completed in the fall of 2009. This green housing project features three-bedroom, two-bathroom, single-family homes, with passive solar, heat-retaining concrete slabs, water harvesting, super-efficient wood stoves, radiant roof barriers, and xeriscape landscaping and rain barrels. Each of the houses was designed, constructed, and furnished with energy efficiency in mind. The entire housing site

Yavapai-Apache housing development in Northern Arizona. (Copyright © Marilyn Angel Wynn/Nativestock.com)

was also laid out with concern for the environment, like the natural watershed and contour of the land in the building of the roads. This project cost about $10 million and was financed by the federal government, a state mortgage finance authority, and the tribe's housing authority.[14] Despite these efforts, the housing shortages persist on all the Apache reservations.

EMPLOYMENT

According to the 2000 U.S. Census, 64.0 percent of all Apache men who were 16 years or older were employed and 54.6 percent of all Apache women also 16 years or older were in the labor force.[15] The median full-time earnings for men were $27,780 and for women it was $22,033. These earnings were substantially below those of all men and women of the U.S. at $37,100 for men and $27,200 for women.[16] Indian people have to pay all federal employment taxes, which are deducted from their paychecks by their employers. Indian employees, like all working Americans, have to file their federal income taxes every April.

The 2000 U.S. Census listed six major categories as the primary areas of occupation for Apache people living on and off their reservations. These six categories were 1) management, professional, and related jobs, 2) the service area, 3) sales and office, 4) farming, fishing, and forestry, 5) construction, extraction, and maintenance, and 6) production, transportation, and material moving. By percentages, 23.7 percent of all Apaches work in management and professional jobs, 24.6 percent in sales and office work, 21.4 percent in the service industry, 13.0 percent in the construction, extraction, and maintenance areas, 15.5 percent in production, transportation, and material moving type jobs, and only 1.8 percent in farming, fishing, and forestry.[17]

While the unemployment rate continues to be high on the Apache Indian reservations, all able-bodied men and women are employed primarily by the tribal government. Employment is also provided by other government agencies, like state government agencies such as the state highway departments and the state public schools. Another source of employment is the U.S. government's Bureau of Indian Affairs and its agencies and departments. The majority of these jobs are in management and administration, from clerical and maintenance staff to middle and top management. Many of the tribes offer summer employment programs to their students.

Since the burgeoning of Indian gaming facilities, the tribal casinos have offered new avenues for employment. With the revenue from the casino, Apache tribes have expanded their enterprises and businesses both on and off the reservation lands, thus providing more employment for their members and nonmembers. In 2000 the average per capita income, the unemployment rate, and number in the tribal labor force of the Apache people by tribe were as follows:

Chart 4.2
Tribal Labor Force

	2000 Per Capita Income	Unemployment Rate	Total Labor Force
Camp Verde	$8,347.00	12.66%	237
Fort Apache	Not available	22.46%	3,696
Tonto Apache	$11,258.00	6.00%	50
San Carlos	$5,200.00	35.42%	2,679
Jicarilla Apache	$10,136.00	14.20%	1,051
Mescalero Apache	$8,118.00	16.00%	2,083
Apache Tribe (OK)	$15,389.00	7.90%	45
Fort Sill Apache	Not available	Not available	4,849

Source: Compiled from tribal profiles in *Tiller's Guide to Indian Country: Economic Profiles of American Indian Reservations*, 2005 edition.

The modern Apache family obtains wages and income from employment. The same kinds of monthly household expenses that face the average U.S. family also face the modern Apache family. Groceries are usually purchased from grocery stores on Indian reservations or from nearby off-reservation towns. The costs of food and fuel on Indian reservations are slightly higher than most larger towns and cities. Furniture and appliances are purchased with cash, credit cards, or through a payment plan if a person qualifies through commercial financing, available in bigger towns close to the Indian reservations, like Farmington, Santa Fe, and Albuquerque, New Mexico; Pagosa Springs, Colorado; and Flagstaff, Phoenix, and Tucson, Arizona. All Apache homes have the same modern amenities, like appliances, telephones, televisions and radios, computers, and access to telecommunications for computers and cable television and cell towers for cell phones. All modern conveniences are available to all Apache people and the standard of living is dependent on their personal preferences and levels of income.

The service industry on the Jicarilla Apache Reservation represents a substantial percentage of tribal employment. All businesses located within the town of Dulce are tribally owned. The newly built and modern Jicarilla Apache Supermarket has a deli-café, a bakery, a Wells Fargo Bank branch, and a community meeting room. A new hardware store affiliated with True Value also opened in 2004. Apache House of Liquors, a Conoco station with a convenience store, the Jicarilla station, and the Best Western Jicarilla Inn are long-standing businesses. The inn offers excellent accommodations, with a restaurant and lounge, and a gift shop with original arts and crafts. The tribe also operates the Jicarilla Shopping Center and the Willow Creek Ranch.[18]

The Mescalero Apache Tribe offers employment in several sectors of its tribal government, including forestry and natural resources, social services, law enforcement, roads, recreation, and administration. In 2005, the Inn of the Mountain Gods Resort employed 355 people, both Apaches and non-Indians, who provide various types of services on a seasonal basis. Ski Apache, the tribal ski resort, also employed 350 people during the ski season. Mescalero Forest Products employed 89 people in a range of job positions from the manufacturing of lumber to the office administrative staff. The BIA agency employed 79 people, mainly in clerical and administrative positions, on the reservation. The on-reservation Indian Health Service clinic employs 68 people, from the physicians to the maintenance personnel.

The federal government employs San Carlos tribal members in the delivery of health, education, and economic services. Tribal enterprises and the tribal government employ many more tribal members. The retail sector, including two convenience stores, a supermarket, a gas station, and a coin-operated laundromat, offers some employment. The San Carlos Unified School District also provides employment. Major private enterprises on the San Carlos Reservation are the Apache Gold Casino (employing more than 400 people, the majority of whom are not Apache people), Apache Timber Products, Basha's, Noline's Country Store, and the San Carlos Lake Development Corporation. Primary public employers include the BIA (employing over 100 people), the Indian Health Service (employing over 150), Rice School District, and the San Carlos Apache Tribe. Many Apaches work off the reservation in neighboring Globe, Fort Thomas, and Safford, Arizona. As home to one of the largest groups of Southwest forest fire fighters, the San Carlos Apache Reservation deploys over 1,000 trained men and women during periods of national emergency.

Service and retail industries on the Fort Apache Reservation offer employment to tribal members. The tribally owned Apache Enterprises operates several convenience markets, grocery stores, and gas stations, including Hon Dah Restaurant, Apache Service Station, Corrizo Food Store, Cedar Creek Food Store, and Seven Mile Food Store. Outdoor and wildlife recreation is a prominent industry on all New Mexico and Arizona Apache reservations. Many Apache men and women make a living as service providers, hunting and fishing guides, and maintenance people in this industry.

EDUCATION

Assimilation Policies and Education

The Dawes Act of 1887 mandated that Native Americans assimilate into U.S. society by becoming private land-owning farmers. This was to be achieved through the allotment of their tribal lands into 160-acre plots. Fortunately for the Arizona and New Mexico Apaches, their tribal lands were not allotted, with the exception of the Jicarilla Apaches. Their lands were allotted in the 1890s but due to mismanagement by the government, the allotments were never individually assigned, and allotment was abandoned in 1937, when all lands were returned to tribal ownership. In general, Apache reservation lands were too arid for farming and lacked adequate water resources. The Apaches were also uncooperative and preferred livestock that required large ranges. Besides, all the arable lands had already been settled and claimed by non-Indians prior to the settlement of the Apaches on the reservations. The remoteness of their reservations was a blessing in disguise when it came to allotment of lands for purposes of farming.

To support its assimilation policy, the federal government assumed responsibility for the education of Indian children in alliance with religious organizations, who shared the vision of civilizing and Christianizing the Indians. Education became the chief instrument for "re-making" the Indians. Congress had promised to provide schools but before the 1890s no serious efforts were made to keep these promises on the Apache reservations. Indian boarding schools were established on the Apache reservations between 1895 and the early 1920s. The first boarding schools were established in 1884 in Mescalero and in 1903 on the Jicarilla Apache Reservation. By 1887, the government had ordered that all instruction in the Indian schools be in English. Apache children were punished for using their own language even at play. In 1892, Congress authorized the Commissioner of Indian Affairs to make school attendance compulsory, and to refuse food rations to families who did not send their children to school.

Education was slow in coming to the Apache reservations, except for the Chiricahua Apache children, who had been shipped with their parents, who were prisoners of war, to Florida and Alabama. In 1879 Captain Richard Henry Pratt inaugurated the federal educational program by establishing the Indian Industrial School at Carlisle, Pennsylvania, where the Chiricahua children were taken. Committed to absolute assimilation, Pratt was credited with making the infamous comments that "the only good Indian is a dead one," and "Kill the Indian in him, and save the man."[19] In this alien environment, many Chiricahua children died from diseases, and many other physical maladies and mental disorders that afflict young children who are separated from their families. During the summer months, the students were not allowed to go home to their parents; instead they were "farmed" out to the families in the area to learn to be farmers and, of course, to provide free labor.

The model established by Pratt became the national model for the Indian boarding school educational programs, where the students attended classes for half a day and worked at the school for the other half of the day.

At the schools, the students typically wore military uniforms, marched to class, were forbidden to speak their native languages, and attended mandatory

Christian services. The schools were often underfunded and were supported in part by the work of the children. The boys worked cleaning, constructing buildings, planting and harvesting food crops, caring for farm animals, digging wells, or quarrying stones, and making shoes, boots and wagons. The girls were responsible for sewing, repairing, washing, and ironing clothing; cooking; and cleaning for the whole school. These chores were in addition to their schoolwork. In fact students spent more hours working in every day than they spent learning in the classroom.[20]

The intent was to provide practical industrial training. Off-reservation Indian boarding schools were established in Albuquerque in 1884 and in Santa Fe and Phoenix in 1890, where the Carlisle model was duplicated and where some Apache children were sent.

The Impact of the Boarding School Experience

There were both positive and negative impacts from the Indian boarding school experiences that Apache Indians have been confronted with since the 1890s. The devastating impact of the forced separation of children from parents has been long term. Nine months out of the year the children from ages 5 to 18 were in the care of boarding school staff. It caused the breakup of family units and ties. Several generations of children were institutionalized, raised without the benefit of the care and love that parents should give to their children. The long-term effects of this institutionalization is still not completely known, but psychologists, sociologists, and historians have referred to it as "historical trauma" and linked it to the high rates of alcoholism, the lack of parental skills, incidence of domestic violence, and the feelings of shame and anger that have plagued the Apache people for many generations.[21]

The positive impact of the boarding school system was that the children were taught the English language, provided with education, and introduced to white society. It was at the Indian boarding schools that the children learned to farm, keep a household, to go to church, how to dress like other Americans, and social manners required by U.S. society. Since the Apache people were so poverty-stricken, the boarding schools at least afforded the children with a roof over their heads and food in their stomachs. The price that was paid by the Apache people was the damage and in some cases outright loss of their religious, language, and cultural knowledge, their pride as Apaches, and ability to be self-determined as a people.

In 1926 federal Indian educational policies took a positive turn when the BIA was investigated and findings published in the Merriam Report of 1928. This report criticized and condemned how the Bureau of Indian Affairs operated the Indian boarding schools. It found overcrowded living conditions, inadequate food and nutrition, lack of proper medical care that often lead to the spread of diseases, and the merciless use of child labor. The Merriam Report led to the New Deal policies that laid the foundation for new Indian educational policies. Children were given enough food and the use of their labor was reduced. Curriculum changes were introduced that eliminated the overwhelming emphasis on white society, on industrial training, the incessant assault on Indian culture, and the interference with Indian religious practices.[22]

The Johnson-O'Malley Act of 1937 authorized the Secretary of Interior to negotiate contracts with the various states to provide public education for Indian students. Most states applied for the funding but did nothing to forward the education of Indian children. It was not until the late 1960s that Indian tribes discovered that the act provided funds for education programs for Indian children attending public schools. In that decade, Indian leaders and organizations focused their attack on the federal government to improve the quality of education, funding for the public schools, and to have parental involvement, including the review of Johnson-O'Malley budgets.

In 1965, the Elementary and Secondary Education Act was passed to meet the special educational needs of low-income families, a category which included almost all Indians. The pressure on the federal government reached another level with a special Senate subcommittee study entitled: *A National Tragedy—A National Challenge* that showed that education for Indians had not improved significantly since the publication of the Merriam Report in 1928. The Indian Education Act of 1972 was the response to this study, and one that ensured Indian control of education and encouraged parent and community participation. The act mandated that until the parent advisory committees formulate the plans and draw up and approve projects and budgets, a school district cannot apply for federal funds. The act also created a national advisory council to consult with and advise the U.S. Office of Indian Education, also established in 1972.[23]

Modern Reservation Education

In the late 1950s, the states of Arizona and New Mexico began establishing public school districts on the Apache Reservations. The states supplemented federal monies channeled through the Johnson-O'Malley Act of 1937 for the cost of education on Indian reservations from state appropriations. To standardize all state school educational curriculums, the Indian boarding schools' curriculums were replaced by the public school curriculum consisting of regular subjects like math, English, science, and social studies. Like all students in the statewide public schools, Apache students had to meet academic requirements to graduate from high school. Transferring the responsibility of education to the public school districts did not mean that the Indian boarding schools were immediately closed. Schools run by the Bureau of Indian Affairs continue on several reservations even today. On the Jicarilla Apache Reservation, for example, students continued to live on the boarding school campus and attended the nearby public schools until the early 1970s. In that decade, all students attended school from their homes.

Today, the majority of Apache students attend public schools, either those located right on the reservation, or in nearby off-reservation towns and communities. Reservation communities are, by and large, located around the Bureau of Indian Affairs agency offices and tribal headquarters, so many students are brought to school by their parents. Buses are provided to students living in distant communities, like on the Fort Apache and San Carlos reservations. The school facilities and equipment are almost all state-of-the art. A typical high school has sufficient classrooms, libraries, computer labs, audio-visual facilities, gymnasiums, playgrounds, football and track fields, teachers' lounges, nurses' offices, and administrative offices. Teachers are mostly non-Indian, however, there is an increase in the number of Apache who are becoming teachers. Head Start programs did not become available until about the late 1970s and, today, all schools have Head Start programs.

On the Yavapai-Apache Reservation, education is available from preschool through high school in the Payson Unified School District. Preschool is also available through the tribe's Head Start program at Camp Verde and at Cottonwood. On the Tonto Apache Reservation, elementary and high school students attend local public schools, and college courses are available from nearby Yavapai College and Eastern Arizona College, both located in Payson, and Pima Community College currently has a satellite learning facility there. On the Fort Apache Reservation at Old Fort Apache is the Theodore Roosevelt School, originally built as a BIA school, which operates today as a boarding and day school and serves approximately 100 Native American students. At Whiteriver, there are two public elementary schools, one junior high school, and a high school. In 2000 there were 4,407 American Indian students attending the Whiteriver Unified District.[24] There are also three BIA schools and a Lutheran mission school on this reservation. There is a branch of Northland Pioneer College at Whiteriver.

The San Carlos Unified School District offers education from K–12 for the San Carlos Apaches. In 2000 that district reported that it had 1,808 American Indians attending its schools.[25] Tuition assistance for college-bound students is available through the tribe's education department, and the adult education program offers post–high school opportunities geared toward trade skills for students seeking training and employment programs. Adult education and GED preparation is also provided through the education department.

In New Mexico, the Jicarilla and Mescalero Apache Tribes send their children to public schools in Dulce, Tularosa, and Ruidoso. The Tularosa Municipal Schools, in Otero County, reported in 2000 that 1,162 American Indians attended their schools, while the Ruidoso Municipal Schools reported 258 students.[26] The Dulce Independent Schools on the Jicarilla Apache Reservation also reported in 2000 that 938 of their students were American Indians.[27] Since only the Mescalero and Jicarilla Apache people live in these areas, it is safe to assume that the majority of American Indian students there are Apaches.

Higher education was not an option on the Apache reservations until the late 1960s. Graduating from high school was still rare in the early 1960s. A small number of Apaches who attended the off-reservation Indian boarding schools in Phoenix, Santa Fe, and Albuquerque graduated from high school, and some of these students went into trade and technical schools. Very few students went on to colleges and universities. Funding was not available until federal funding was provided through the Bureau of Indian Affairs higher education programs in the 1960s. Several of the tribes also began assisting their students with higher education funding. In 1952, the Jicarilla Apache Tribe established the $1 million Chester E. Faris Scholarship fund from the first proceeds from the discovery of oil and gas on the southern portion of its reservation, but it was not used until the 1960s. Tribal members could use the funds for either technical training or attending colleges and universities. A decade later the first Apache students began entering graduate schools and receiving their advanced degrees.

Since the 1980s the Apache tribes have established tribal education departments to assist their members with all types of educational programs. Managing higher education programs—from assisting students with college applications and finding outside funding sources, to keeping track of the students through college to determine their continuing eligibility for financial assistance—is the number one reason for their existence. In addition to administering college-related programs, they also offer opportunities and services geared toward obtaining trade skills for students seeking technical training and employment programs. An array of community educational programs are also offered by these departments, like adult education that focuses on post–high school training and employment programs, preparation for the GED, and language and cultural preservation programs. Services offered are computer labs, libraries, and development of cultural curriculum

Chart 4.3
Education Attainment (According to the 2000 U.S. Census)

	High School Graduation or Higher	Bachelor's Degree or Higher
Camp Verde	54.5%	8.2%
Fort Apache	54.3%	6.3%
Tonto Apache	76.3%	6.0%
San Carlos	57.6%	2.8%
Jicarilla Apache	77.6%	13.9%
Mescalero Apache	72.6%	6.4%
Apache Tribe (OK)	74.6%	6.4%
Fort Sill Apache	Not available	15.7%

Source: Compiled from tribal profiles in *Tiller's Guide to Indian Country: Economic Profiles of American Indians*, 2005 edition.

materials, summer camp programs, recreation programs, video documentation, and after-school tutoring. These programs are not always offered on a consistent basis, depending on the funding and personnel.

The modern Apache lifestyle, for all practical purposes, is similar to the lifestyle in small town America. The exception is that small town America has always kept up with modern lifestyles and trends throughout the country. They have not made a shift in their lifestyle from dire poverty to a more standard way of life just within the last few decades. Rural America is not totally dependent on the federal government for its standard of living, the quality of its housing, nor the education of its children. With the revenue from Indian gaming, Apache tribes now have the resources to enter into partnerships with the states, private companies, and various agencies of the federal government to build and improve their communities.

Notes

1. "Most Populous Indian Reservations, 2000," http://www.infoplease.com/ipa/A0922239.html (accessed March 23, 2010).

2. U.S. Census Bureau, American FactFinder, "New Mexico–American Indian Area, GCT-PH1.Population, Housing Units, Area, and Density: 2000," http://www.factfinder.census.gov (accessed March 23, 2010).

3. U.S. Census Bureau, "Figure 1. Selected Age Groups and Median Age: 2000," *We the People: American Indians and Alaska Natives in the United States*, Census 2000 Special Reports (U.S. Department of Commerce, February 2006).

4. U.S. Census Bureau, 2004 American Community Survey, Selected Population Profiles, "Table 2. American Indian and Alaska Native Household Population by Tribal Group: 2004," *The American Community—American Indians and Alaska Natives: 2004*, 2.

5. Portions of pages 4 to 7 previously published in Veronica E. Tiller, Compiler, *Tiller's Guide to Indian Country: Economic Profiles of American Indian Reservations* (Albuquerque: BowArrow Publishing, 2005). Reprinted with permission.

6. Indian Health Service, "Facts on Indian Health Disparities, January 2006," http://info.ihs.gov/Files/DisparitiesFacts-Jan2006.pdf (accessed March 30, 2010).

7. Portions of pages 8 to 14 previously published in *Tiller's Guide*, Reprinted with permission.

8. U.S. Bureau of the Census, Statistical Brief, Housing of American Indians on Reservations—Structural Characteristics, 1990, http://www.ewebtribe.com/NACulture/articles/IndianHousingStats.htm (accessed March 30, 2010).

9. U.S. Census Bureau, *We the People*, "Figure 2. Household Type and Average Household Size: 2000.*"

10. U.S. Census Bureau, American FactFinder, "New Mexico–American Indian Area, GCT-PH1.Population, Housing Units, Area, and Density: 2000," http://www.factfinder.census.gov (accessed March 23, 2010).

11. National American Indian Housing Council, "Indian Housing Fact Sheet," http://www.naihc.net/news/index.asp?bid=6316 (accessed March 29, 2010).

12. "White Mountain Apache Housing Authority - Apache Dawn," in http://www.wmtnaha.com/index.php?option=com_content&task=view&id=20&ltemid=37 (accessed March 22, 2010).

13. *Tiller's Guide*, 291.

14. "Mescalero Apache Housing Is First 'Fully Green' Project," *New Mexico Business Weekly*, Friday, August 7, 2007 in http://www.albuquerque.bizjournals.com/albuquerque/stories/2009/08/10/story10.html (accessed March 22, 2010).

15. U.S. Census Bureau, *We the People*, "Figure 5. Labor Force Participation by Sex: 2000," 9.

16. U.S. Census Bureau, *We the People*, "Figure 7. Median Earnings by Sex: 2000," 11.

17. U.S. Census Bureau, *We the People*, "Figure 8. Poverty Rate: 1999," 12.

18. Portions of pages 20 to 21 previously published in *Tiller's Guide*. Reprinted with permission.

19. Donald E. Worcester, *The Apaches: Eagles of the Southwest* (Norman: University of Oklahoma Press, 1979), 329–330.

20. Arlene Hirschfelder and Martha Kreipe de Montaño, The Native American Almanac: A Portrait of Native America Today (New York: Prentice Hall Genral Reference, 1993), 95.

21. "Historical Trauma May Be Causing Today's Health Crisis," *Indian Country Diaries*, http://www.pbs.org/indiancountry/challenges/trauma.html (accessed March 23, 2010); Maria Yellow Horse Brave Heart, and Lemyra M. DeBruyn, Ph.D. "The American Indian Holocaust: Healing Historical Unresolved Grief," http://aianp.uchsc.edu/journal/pdf/8(2)_4_YellowHorseBraveHeart_American_Indian_holocaust.pdf. (accessed March 23, 2010).

22. Worcester, *The Apaches*, 333.

23. Ibid., 337.

24. "Whiteriver Unified District, Navajo County, Arizona," School District Demographics System—Race and Ethnicity Profile, http://www.nces.ed.gov/surveys/sdds/pfethnicityone.asp?state1=4&county1=0409160 (accessed February 22, 2010).

25. "San Carlos Unified School District," School District Demographics.

26. "Tularosa Municipal Schools, Otero County and Ruidoso Municipal Schools, Lincoln County," School District Demographics.

27. "Dulce Independent Schools, Rio Arriba County," School District Demographics.

5

Social Customs, Gender Roles, Marriage, Children, and Cuisine

THE PERSISTENCE OF APACHE CULTURE from ancient times to modern times is a theme that still governs social customs, the family, and even the food that is eaten; however, it is recognized that the influences of the dominant society have been the agent of social change in Apache society. Apache people have selected and adopted those elements of social change that they were willing to accept and rejected those that they did not want or like. In many cases, they were forced to accept the ways of U.S. society, but even those were modified. In short, they have a homogenized or mixed society consisting of Apache and U.S. ways.

SOCIAL CUSTOMS

Any discussion concerning Apache social customs cannot occur without taking a look at traditions of the past as well as the practices of today. The social customs of the past have survived in many respects; some have merged with present customs and others have been replaced by social customs of the dominant U.S. society. Today, by and large, there is a blending of the past with the present.

In general, Apaches are respectful and reserved. When they see each other they acknowledge each other with subtle salutations, perhaps a nod and a warm smile. Men may shake hands, women and children may hug each other, but usually there are no loud expressions of greetings, salutations, and kissing in public. It is not an Apache custom to be loud, flamboyant, and overexpressive. It is acceptable to greet another person or group by saying *hello*, *hi*, *greetings*, and by shaking hands or hugging, as in the way other Americans usually greet each other.

Family Gatherings

Community life is important, and Apaches enjoy social gatherings, celebrations, ceremonies, sporting events, and parties. Prior to the 1970s, when most Apache families were spread out across the reservation rather than in the tribal-headquarters town or village, Apaches enjoyed visiting each other. Often a family—especially a family within an extended family—visited with another family or friends for several days at a time. During this time, the host family would feed and house the visiting family. Most Apache families lived in rural areas and communities where livestock was raised, along with crops and gardens. Visits might require butchering a sheep or gathering more food from the garden. Children particularly enjoyed visiting their friends and relatives. Children would gather to play games, pretend to camp out, have horse and foot races, and play with the pets, dolls, and toys. At these family gatherings, children were expected to assist with any household tasks and chores that each of the host family's children had to do, including the care of livestock. During these visits, the adults also visited, shared stories, gossiped, talked about tribal affairs, upcoming elections, marriages, and upcoming feasts and ceremonies. Extended visiting among families and friends was a social custom that kept families together. It was very important for all members of a family to know who their relatives were, and this was one way to have family get-togethers and renew family ties.

Today these family gatherings continue, but under different circumstances. Family gatherings are now centered on U.S. holidays, like Thanksgiving, Christmas, and the Fourth of July, and special events, birthday parties, anniversaries, graduations, and funerals. These family gatherings are very similar to social gatherings in the dominant society. Birthdays are popular times for family gatherings. Fast food like hot dogs and hamburgers, potato chips, and soft drinks are usually the kind of food served at birthday parties, along with a birthday cake and ice cream.

Gift Giving

Guests and family members are expected but not required to bring gifts appropriate for the age of the birthday person. Gifts can be expensive or reasonable. Children's birthdays are celebrated for fun and to acknowledge the children for all the good things they have done, the challenges they have overcome, and to wish them another good year. Adults celebrate their

Vigil family celebrating Robert's 11th birthday. (Courtesy of Bobbie Nell Vigil)

birthdays for fun and as an occasion to have a gathering for family and friends. Elder's birthdays are for celebrating their longevity and for honoring them for the role they play in the family. In many ways, birthdays for elders have replaced the old practice of respecting and honoring the elders, since the families today may be more apart and separated than in the past.

Gift giving has always been an Apache custom. It was customary for grand-parents to give children gifts ranging from telling them special stories, singing songs for them, cooking special meals for them, teaching them new skills, and going on special walks, to giving them jewelry when they become older teen-agers, and blankets and household goods to their married children. Grand-children always gave gifts to their grandparents and parents by making them proud of their accomplishments, having good manners, being kind and generous, and by presenting them with material gifts. It was also custom-ary for visitors to leave with some kind of gift, whether of food, supplies or materials like beads, arts and crafts, or store-bought goods and products.

Gift giving was a custom of showing gratitude for the abundance and goodness one received from the universe. Apaches believed that the more one gave, the more one received, but a gift was not given with an expectation of getting something in return, otherwise it was not gratitude but an act of calculated reciprocity. Gift giving was not confined just for special occasions, either, but gifts were given year around. Today, gift giving is done mainly on birthdays, anniversaries, and special events like graduation from high school or college, marriage, and at Christmas.

Apache Tribal Gatherings

Most Apache tribal gatherings are centered on events such as the puberty feasts, Gah Dances, and other tribal ceremonies. Usually these events take place in the rural areas of the reservation and require the host families to camp out. Camping out for the ceremonies and feasts are major events and undertakings. As such, these ceremonies cost a lot of money to stage and require the families to pool their money or save their monies over a period of time just to buy the food. For the Jicarilla Apaches, when there is a puberty ceremony it requires a family to have enough food to feed the entire tribe for four days, to have water and wood on hand for cooking and fuel, and to have a sufficient labor force to feed the people, set up the camp, and take down the camp. It is customary for the extended family and friends to devote lots of planning time to these events. In many tribes, the families are given time off from their jobs to attend to these cultural affairs. These events are fun for younger children, older children, and adults to get together and socialize. The puberty feasts were the main social events for tribal members in traditional times. To stage a feast required the entire family and its resources. Family members all brought food of one kind or another and offered their labor and enjoyed themselves. It is a long-standing custom that when a family has a puberty feast, the entire family is to offer their help and resources.

Religious ceremonies are also gatherings for families and friends. In these instances there are many pre-planning meetings among the men and women who are in charge of the ceremonies. They set out certain rules and procedures for the conduct of the ceremonies, usually long-standing customs that have to be followed. There are many social and religious taboos that have to be observed. For example, a cigarette is placed on a medicine person's right foot as a request for his or her services. If he or she picks up the cigarette, that signifies acceptance. It is also a custom to pay for services of the medicine men; in traditional times a medicine man or woman could be given the surplus food from the feast or any livestock that was not slaughtered. The medicine men or women accepted whatever was offered to them. Today, medicine persons are usually paid in cash. The ceremonies also require not only that there is sufficient food, but that all ceremonial items are collected and ready for use prior to the start of the ceremony. In the case of the puberty feasts, the women are in charge of the girl's care and well-being. It is expected that everyone work together to carry out the feast.

Everyone, without exception, is welcomed at the feast and given as much food as they will eat. They are also welcome to take home some food. It is the belief of the tribe that the feast does not belong to any one family; that the purpose of the feast is for the entire tribe, and no one can be turned away. Everyone is expected to behave in a respectful way, and if they do not, they are asked to leave. Non-Apache visitors, who are usually the guests of Apache tribal members, are welcomed and treated with respect but are expected to remain outside the ceremonial tepee unless specifically invited by the medicine person or host family. Taking of pictures is prohibited for both members and non-tribal members. The food is usually blessed at the beginning of the ceremony or feast and does not have to be done at every meal. At the blessing, everyone stands and gives their full attention to the person giving the prayer of thanks to the Creator and Mother Earth. These days, some of the prayers are given in English in the Christian way.

Social Relations

Interpersonal relations are characterized by a code of behavior that places emphasis on respect. Elders are not only respected but have a special position within Apache society.[1] It is the elders who are the keepers of tribal wisdom and knowledge, which they are charged with passing down to the next generation. In any social gatherings the elders always speak first, are first to be seated at the dining tables, and are the first to be served. It is usually the most elderly at any gathering that has the first right to say the prayers. The younger people are expected to give up their seats, offer food and refreshments, and assist with anything that the elders may request or need. Failure to show respect for elders is not only a sign of bad manners but can stigmatize a family or ruin a family's reputation. It is often said that when one does not know his or her traditional ways, or the ways of the tribe, that he or she must have no grandparents. All elders are usually addressed as grandmother or grandfather regardless of whether or not they are actually closely related to a person. Grandparents are to be spoken to not only politely but in a way that shows endearment. For example, a grandmother may be addressed in Apache as "my dear little grandmother" to show endearment. Today, the social conventions require that the elderly be addressed as Mr. or Mrs. by their last names.

In traditional Apache society elders were always taken care of in their old age and were never separated from their families. They were valued members of the family and not seen as burdens. In other words, there was no such thing as separate homes for elders. However, today in modern society, Apache tribes have adopted the dominant society's ways of caring for their elderly, and many elders are now placed in senior care centers and homes for the elderly.

Respect for elders is a key social custom among the Apaches. The culture of respect and honor for elders goes back to the Creation stories. One must respect what preceded one or what brought one into this world, whether it is ancestral man and woman, the animals, the celestial beings, or the land and the environment. One cannot exist with those that came before. It is the elders who have the experience, the wisdom, and the knowledge. To earn the respect and honor, the elders have social responsibilities, like sharing their experiences, passing down the wisdom, and being knowledgeable. In the old days, it was the grandparents who were charged with the education of the children. They made sure the children knew about their religion, their social customs, who and how they were related to the extended family and tribe, and about their environment. Today, elders as a class in society are given respect and honor, but as individuals, it cannot be assumed they earned the respect. They have to have lived a life that accords respect and honor. So if an elder lived a dishonorable life, then he or she cannot expect undue respect and honor.

Social customs are based on sharing and generosity, honesty and integrity, respect for all living things, spirituality, and love for family and tribe. Sharing and generosity are two Apache customs that have both a philosophical basis as well as a practical one. Perhaps the best expression of sharing is inviting everyone to share in a meal no matter the amount or type of food. If there are ten people and there is only one pot of soup, everyone gets his or her share. It is considered extremely rude and ill mannered to eat in front of someone and not invite him or her to share in the food. Children are brought up with the notion that they have to share with their siblings. From sharing comes the related idea of generosity. It does not matter what station in life one is in, that person can be generous with his or her time, love and affections, open-mindedness, leadership skills, ideas, and support for others. If a person is financially successful, he or she is expected to share the wealth and to be a generous person. One cannot have social status because of one's wealth if that person is selfish. The survival of the tribe is based on the idea of sharing with all the people and being generous towards each other.

Like eating but not inviting someone to eat with you, not offering help when someone needs it is considered rude and uncouth. This is especially true when young folks are in the company of elders. Having the ability to work well, efficiently, and with a good attitude is highly valued. Apache women pride themselves with their ability to work as well as the men. Feigning helplessness is not an admired trait among Apache women, but this is never an excuse for the men to stand by while women are working, especially when the work involves physical strength.

While, historically, there have always been social distinctions between social classes, such as between medicine men, chiefs, warriors, and other highly respected elders, Apache society is basically egalitarian, democratic, and socialistic. It has been recognized that the survival of the tribe was more important than the individual. In traditional societies, it was the common religion and the common language that held the tribal society together. Within the tribes there were extended family groupings that were basically independent from each other. They lived together in localized areas where they shared food resources, protected each other, socialized with each other, raised children together, and worked together. Each group had its own leader who was not obligated to one tribal leader. The concept of one supreme ruler, like a king or president, was foreign. It was not political organizations, units, or philosophies that brought traditional families together, it was usually their religion or their religious views and practices. This is not to say that there were not reasons for Apaches to get together in times of war, famine, or for common purpose.

The Apache families knew the boundaries of their traditional homelands, and within those boundaries they operated as separate and independent families. They knew their religious stories, philosophies, and worldviews, and how to live within their world. Seemingly, they did not need a political structure, political boundaries, or social or political enforcement. It was not until they were placed on Indian reservations that they began to establish organized political organizations known as tribal councils and tribal governments. The political units created by modern Apache governments were known as districts for purposes of representation on the tribal council. In many instances, the Apache families nearly replicated their family residential patterns upon its tribal governmental districts. In tribal governments, there are council representatives from the family groupings. On the Jicarilla Reservation, there are no longer tribal governmental districts as tribal president, vice president, and councilmen are elected at large. There are still districts on the Fort Apache and San Carlos Reservations from which tribal councilmen and women are elected.

The modern political organizations have required new social customs, but the traditional value of families within the tribal structure has survived the test of time, so that political decisions are made along family lines. It is not unusual for councilmen and women to campaign for office first among family members, then the rest of the tribal voters. It is believed that serving on the tribal council depends, to a large degree, on the size of one's extended family. Once in council, it is not uncommon for council men and women to make decisions like giving a person a job, promoting someone in a tribal department, giving a raise, or giving out benefits based on family ties and considerations. Like all political decisions made within the numerous levels of U.S. government, decisions are made based on one's supporters.

Family continues to be a primary consideration in political decisions. Today on all the large Apache reservations the lands are held in common or under tribal ownership. This is a direct link between how the ownership of land from the past was viewed and how it has survived into modern times. There is no private ownership of lands, although there are land assignments for residential, farming, or ranching purposes. With the exception of the Jicarilla Apache Tribe in New Mexico and the Oklahoma Apache Tribes, there was no individual allotment of tribal lands on the Arizona and New Mexico Reservations under the Dawes Act of 1887, because the people believed that the land had to be held in common despite federal Indian policies. The Jicarilla Apaches never accepted the allotments and by the 1930s all lands reverted back to tribal ownership. The Oklahoma Apache Tribes still have individual allotments of land.

The belief in the importance of the family has also governed modern Apache life. All tribal governmental benefits are to be shared by all tribal members. Whenever the tribe is given federal monies, it is for the entire tribe, and received on behalf of, and for the benefit of, the entire tribe. The belief in ownership in common has thwarted the growth of the private business sector. There are few private businesses owned by Apache tribal members, in favor of tribal ownership of business enterprises.

The Traditional Apache Family

In traditional Apache society, the family, extended family, and the tribe were vitally important in the survival of the Apaches as a people. Social customs originated from religious viewpoints that celebrated all aspects of family, whether it was the family of man and all other living beings or the extended family and the tribe. Social customs and social relationships emerged from religious ceremonies and events that were conducted to preserve and protect the family units within a given physical environment. Current lifestyles and customs reflect the retention of traditional beliefs and practices, as well as their adaptation to changing times and modern society.

The traditional Apache family consisted of the grandfather, the grandmother, their unmarried sons and daughters, married daughters and their husbands, and their children. The size of the extended family depended on the number of married daughters and their husbands and children. When a son married, he usually went to live with his in-laws. Among the Jicarilla Apaches, when the son married into another clan, he and his children became members of the new clan. For instance, if his mother was a member of the Ollero Clan, and he married a Llanero woman, then he joined the Llanero Clan.

In Western society, the nuclear family consists of a father, a mother, and their children. In the traditional Apache society, the family did not center on the nuclear family but on the extended family. The kinship system operated to protect everyone, from the grandparents to the children. Keeping harmony within the extended family was reflected by the relationship between the nuclear and the extended family. Today, this is still practiced to a certain extent. The fathers and mothers become parents for all children of their siblings. All the mothers' sisters become surrogate mothers to all the children and all the fathers' brothers become the surrogate fathers to all the children. The reason for this is so that children were never without parents. When a mother dies, all the surviving sisters become mothers to her children. The same is true when a father dies; the remaining brothers become fathers to the children. All the children become brothers and sisters.

An Apache child's true uncle is his or her mother's brother. The true aunt is the father's sister. The true cousins are the children of the true uncles and aunts. Within this family structure there are "teasing cousins." They are the children of one's uncles, and the girls can tease the girls, and the boys, the boys. Teasing is considered a hurtful and abusive way to treat people. Teasing can cause emotional hurt; it can lead to lack of self-esteem, and it can cause conflict and broken relationships. The Apaches recognize that everyone teases at one time or another. By having a teasing cousin, a person has a way to publicly deal with teasing in a way that everyone knows is only a "social custom license." In Apache society, it is understood that the spoken word is very powerful, so one always has to pay attention and be mindful of what one says. Often people say mean things under the guise of "I am only teasing you" or "I was just teasing." So the Apaches created a way to say things—some mean things, but mostly and mainly, the funny, the ridiculous, the profane, and things that are not otherwise socially allowed. For example, grandparents might blame their teasing cousins for any mistakes they made. Because of the power of the word, a person would not ordinarily refer to the death of another person for fear that it may come true. But it is true that human beings have thoughts of death, and for the Apaches, the teasing cousin relationship provides that outlet. One is allowed to say almost anything about, and to, their teasing cousin and get away with it. In the past, some of the teasing was quite rude, crude, and funny. It also provided a person with a way to take criticism under less traumatic circumstances. It taught a person that one is not the center of the universe; that everything was not about them. It is often difficult to tell someone to curb his or her egotism, but in a teasing way, this message can be made loud and clear. The key to the teasing is that both parties have to understand the meaning of the teasing relationship. Over time, the teasing relationship leads to having a favorite teasing cousin whom one enjoys for a lifetime because it results in understanding, love, and endearment. Today, the role of teasing cousin is not widely practiced nor is it encouraged.

Another valuable Apache social custom that links the past with the present is the respect for the natural environment. Apache people do not engage in "controlling" their natural environment and this is reflected in various ways. For example, the majority of Apache homes do not have lawns that use huge amounts of water. While weeds might be controlled, natural plants are not killed in favor of lawns. Artificial landscaping is not practiced in a wholesale fashion on Apache reservations. Apache tribal governments also do not operate with the notion that the natural landscape has to be developed. Appreciation of the beauty of nature and willingness to let nature take its course are still valued beliefs and customs among Apache people.

GENDER ROLES

Women

Traditional Apache societies were matriarchal. Women were in charge of their households, the raising and protecting of children, the care of the family, making political decisions, serving as medicine people, and honoring their roles as women in general. Historically, the role of Apache women has been devalued and marginalized by the dominant society, which is patriarchal, where the men are the heads of household and women are unequal partners. The assimilation process, especially through Christian churches, preached that men were the proper heads of household and women were to be subservient to their husbands and other males; that children were practically the property of their parents; that lineal descent was through the male line; and all authority, rights, and privileges rested with the male members of society. Even after many generations of exposure to this system, the Apache people have not totally adopted this concept of patriarchy. Apache women today have maintained their role as head of household, despite all the social conventions that they were expected to adopt.

According to Apache religious views, women were always considered as equal partners, that it takes both male and female to make human life possible and that one sex is not dominant at the expense of the other. With this view of life, Apache women assumed the roles of sister, cousin, mother, aunt, wife, and grandmother with reserved confidence and quiet dignity. The precarious economic circumstances which the Apache women found themselves in, those that shattered their traditional societies—the overwhelming and ever-present poverty and the lack of status in a new alien world—required acceptance, patience, and faith. Apache women had no access to modern conveniences, privileges, and comforts afforded to the average non-Indian women in the United States at that time. The new life on the reservation life was hard, often bleak and hopeless. There was no sanctuary, only the drudgery of an antiseptic existence in a new and strange world.

Always up to the challenges of life, Apache women accepted and embraced the idea that eventually all would work out. They continued to keep up appearances of cooperation, but one that bordered on stubborn acquiescence. Despite adversity, her family was still an Apache woman's priority. The quiet and unspoken support from her extended family could still be counted on. Despite that their children were taken from them and placed in a boarding school for nine months of the year, and their men had no visible means to support their families, women continued to believe in their religion, customs, and ways. Women rolled up their sleeves and set up homes that were tepees, shacks, tents, or brush shelters. They smiled and gave thanks for the meager meat ration their husbands brought back from the agency and for the time they were going to spend with their children when summer arrived. When their husbands took up farming, they were right there helping like efficient and well-paid ranch hands without complaint. At the same time they cooked, raised their children, made baskets and other crafts, and helped with the tribal ceremonies, often in secrecy.

Bombarded with social forces beyond their control, Apache women persisted knowing that the survival of their people depended on their individual and collective strength and determination. Along the way, many Apache women accepted Western culture and lifestyles. Women attended school, learned the ways of their white sisters, and tolerated and understood why Apache men more readily accepted the patriarchal system.

Apache women never had an easy life in comparison to women of the dominant society. Faced with economic poverty, high mortality rates, inadequate medical care, poor schooling, and a society that denigrated their people and their person as women, only through their determination, tenacity, creativity, spirituality, and love for their families and tribe were they able to survive in two worlds. Laughter, humor, silliness, giggling, crying, singing, and being happy was part of their behavior and way of being—just not in public, especially in public where there were non-Indians. Apache women outwardly had to be tough and were often portrayed in the media as stern and mean, yet they were kind, loving, caring, sweet, funny—but only in the company of family and close friends. They had the respect of their husbands and family and could be counted on in times of need and in times of crisis to be level-headed and courageous.

Men

In traditional Apache society, men did not compete with women to be the head of household—they had plenty to do as men, like become warriors, leaders, medicine men, and hunters bringing food to their families. They acknowledged the role of women in Apache society as important and one to be respected and honored. In turn, they knew that without honoring and respecting their grandmothers, mothers, and other female members, they were dishonoring themselves as men. Everything worked in balance. If either the men or women could not respect one another, a grave imbalance occurred that would lead to disharmony, conflict, and dysfunction.

Men were, and are, the heads of families in traditional Apache society, as well as in contemporary times, but not for the same reasons attributed to Western patriarchal systems. In Apache society, men and women were equal partners in life, but it was recognized that they had different and important roles in society. Men were given the responsibility to protect their families because they were endowed with greater physical strength than women, enabling them to run faster, longer, and over greater distances. With their physical strength, men could lift heavier loads and even take on an animal with a

Hunting on the Apache reservations is still a favorite activity for fathers, uncles, brothers, sons, and friends. (Courtesy of Fred Vigil)

proper weapon. It took extraordinary physical strength to kill a huge, angry, snorting and running buffalo by accurately shooting an arrow deep into its chest at close range while remaining mounted bareback on a horse that was also running at top speed.

The Creator gave men the role of hunter to provide for their families. A man was given the bow and arrow, which was understood by his society to mean that he was also to be a warrior and protect his family and land from its enemies. War was his domain, as was political leadership for his family and tribe. He was also given the domain of religion. Men were the spiritual leaders, the medicine men, the ceremonial dancers, and it was their role to protect the religion of the people. This did not mean that women could not be medicine women or spiritual leaders, as they too knew the wisdom of the ages and much religious knowledge resided with them.

For all that the men were endowed with and all their political leadership responsibilities, men were not kings, dictators, or privileged tyrants. When a man was given the role as leader of his people, he had to work from a consensus basis, where the entire group's wishes and desires had to be considered. It was his duty to be honest, upstanding, and to act with integrity. Beyond this, he also had the responsibility to help raise his children, care for his parents, and assist with the household chores that required physical strength and stamina. He was viewed as a human with all the frailties and flaws, as well as the good and positive traits. Women honored him because his role as provider and protector was as important as the role of the women in his society.

Today, Apache men are considered the heads of household by U.S. standards and social conventions. Since the establishment of tribal governments in the 1930s, men have been the official tribal leaders, serving as chairman, vice chairman, and councilmen. In the labor force, Apache men are paid more than Apache women. They have a shorter life span than women. In the 2000 U.S. Census, on three of the four Arizona Apache reservations, males were outnumbered by the females.[2]

MARRIAGE

Traditional Apache marriages began with a short courtship. The young couple informed their parents of their intention to marry. If the couple was too closely related, the grandparents usually called off the marriage and the couple had no choice but to go their separate ways. Parents had the right to object to a prospective partner but a couple could technically still get married, just not with the blessing of the families. If the couple met the "requirements," both sets of parents came to an agreement about gifts that the groom was to give to his future in-laws and the "dowry" that the bride was to bring with her. A date was set and a marriage ceremony took place with singing, prayers, feasting, and dancing. A medicine man or woman was hired and conducted the ceremony. The bride and groom dressed in their finest traditional clothing and could exchange vows. The wedding celebration was usually a one-day and one-night affair consisting of feasting and dancing. The couple then set up a household at the bride's parent's home and the groom became a member of his wife's extended family.

Another past marriage practice was the arranged marriage. Usually a male of marrying age could request the help of his parents or relatives to approach the family of the girl to propose a marriage. The family of the girl could accept or decline the offer. If the parents accepted the marriage proposal, then they also requested a gift: a gift of horses, livestock, or anything of value. The girl had some say-so and she was not treated like chattel, but economic circumstances often provided the motivation for the parents' decisions. Often, the young couple had already made the "prior" agreements, and this practice was just going through the motions.

After several generations on the reservation, many families still had traditional wedding ceremonies after the couple had obtained a legal marriage license. Apache families legitimized and protected the institution of marriage and cooperated in getting the proper licenses. In addition, some families got a license and had both a traditional wedding ceremony and a church wedding.

Today, the concept of marriage lacks the significance it had in the previous generations. The social stigmatism that was once attached to being a single female with children or living together as a married couple without the official blessings of families no longer exists, except maybe among the older generations of Apaches. As a result, there is a high rate of single females with children. According the 2000 U.S. Census, out of about 75,000 Apaches, including those that are married to other Indian people or people from other races, 35 percent have never married and about 43 percent are married but separated. The divorce rate is about 14 percent.[3]

In 2000, there were 18,130 households among the Apaches. Of this number, 13,242, or 73 percent, were family households and 4,888, or 27 percent, were non-family households. In 44.1 percent of Apache households there is a married couple with children under 18 years old; another 14 percent is made up of single females with children under 18 years old.[4]

Marriage is still considered a life-changing and life-altering decision for Apache couples. Marriage begins with courtship, and the term of the courtship is up to the couple; it can be many years or a few weeks. There are many occasions and circumstances for teenage boys and girls to get to know each other. The main opportunity was and still is at school. In the days of the Indian boarding school and today in high school and in college, teenagers and young adults have numerous opportunities for finding marriage partners. Dating is a social institution that has been accepted and adopted on Apache reservations. It has traditionally been the role of the male partner to propose a marriage, but today females can also propose a marriage.

In general, Apache women see marriage as a positive and desirable institution. Being married and having children is a desirable goal toward which to strive. Having children is viewed as a wonderful reason for living. For those Apaches who believe in their traditional ways, the puberty feasts and ceremonies are celebrated to announce to the world that the girl is now a woman and ready to take on her role as partner in marriage and as a mother. Apache mothers have always encouraged their daughters to marry and have done whatever it takes to have their daughters marry in the most advantageous ways and for the right reasons. Topping the list of the right reasons are love and respect for each other.

There are Apache customs that are still taken into consideration even though they are no longer the norm or the rule. Marrying a close relative is still forbidden in many families. Marrying too young or marrying for the "wrong reasons" is frowned upon. The wrong reasons could be an unwanted pregnancy, an abusive and coercive relationship, to get out of other commitments, because it seemed like something to do, or because of peer or parental pressure.

The common-law marriage is an unspoken and accepted way for Apache people to get married. Common-law marriages are the norm on Apache reservations. Under this type of marriage, couples do not bother with weddings, they simply move in together and start "being married." Soon, everyone gets the idea and accepts the marriage. This type of marriage occurs without the fanfare, the public announcements, and the expense of a wedding, perhaps to keep it a private matter, or as a way to test the couple's commitment to each other. Young couples move in together, most likely into the homes of their parents. Eventually they move into their own homes.

Often these couples have children and later may obtain a legal marriage license. This type of marriage has led to a high rate of single female heads of household, where there is no father. It has also led to a high rate of separation and divorce. In 2004, about 42 percent of American Indians and Alaska Natives aged 15 and older were married, compared with about 57 percent of non-Hispanic whites aged 15 and older. American Indians and Alaska Natives (about 35%) were more likely than non-Hispanic whites (about 24%) never to have married. About one of every six American Indians and Alaska Natives was either separated (about 3%) or divorced (about 14 %), compared with about one of every eight non-Hispanic whites (about 2% and about 11%, respectively).[5]

Interracial marriages among the Apaches are common today. Apaches marry other Indians from other tribes and people from all other races. In

2000 there were about 57,000 Apaches who claimed only one tribe, whereas there were approximately another 47,000 Apaches who were either married to a person from another tribe or another race. One reason for marrying outside the tribe is because the eligible marriage pool may be too small. Students who go off to college often marry other Indians or non-Indians. These marriages are accepted just like other tribal marriages. Apache people live too far apart for finding other Apaches to marry. Proximity still governs when it comes to finding a marriage partner. The Apaches of Arizona are closer together than they are to the New Mexico and Oklahoma Apaches and perhaps there are greater chances of marriage among the Arizona Apache tribes, particularly the White Mountain and San Carlos.

CHILDREN

When former first lady Hilary Clinton said that it takes a village to raise a child, the advocates for families and children raised their glasses as if this was a Newtonian discovery. The Apaches have always known that "it takes a tribe to raise a child." Children are at the other end of the family spectrum from the grandparents. To an Apache who has had the luxury and blessing to have

Halloween is a fun time for Apache children. (Courtesy of Bobbie Nell Vigil)

or to have had grandparents, there is no better relationship. Life without grandparents is like being a bird without wings. Grandparents are the source of all tribal wisdom and knowledge, from philosophical and religious matters to learning to tie one's shoes.

The teaching of children in traditional society is shared. Teaching becomes an easy task with children with numerous fathers and mothers. If a female child has four aunts, imagine her access and resources for learning about the arts, medicinal plants and herbs, raising children, dealing with one's relationships, etc. Usually, no one person has all the knowledge about any one subject, but a group can serve as a knowledge "pool." This was what was available to an Apache child from his or her extended family. Learning is a lifetime endeavor. One learns various things at different times from different family members. There are several important things that an Apache learns. One is having reverence for the Sacred Universe and Apache religion. Usually this is taught by the grandparents and reinforced by the adult relatives.

In traditional Apache society children were raised to have respect for elders, to respect the ways of the Apache people, and to have respect for the environment and all living things. All these values and behaviors were taught through everyday activities, through oral histories, and through religious activities and ceremonies. Children were seen as valuable members of society. They entered the world with a ceremony of thanks to the Creator. The raising of children was a responsibility shared by all members of the extended family. A child was never to be left alone. Brothers and sisters had the same responsibilities for the care of their baby siblings as the mother. They were to watch the babies, play with them, and sing to them, especially when they became toddlers. Like adults, they were to teach their young siblings all that they knew. Within a few weeks after birth, the Apache families conducted a ceremony that took various forms, like having a medicine person bless and bathe the baby. The boy or girl infant was given a first pair of moccasins and a blanket.

Throughout the life of an Apache, special ceremonies are held to commemorate the end of one stage of life and the beginning of the next phase. As a toddler, both the boy and girl had their hair shaven off to symbolize the end of infancy and the beginning of the next stage of life. This mini-ceremony is no longer practiced. Teenage girls have the puberty feast to celebrate the beginning of womanhood. Young boys are also initiated into the ceremonies like the Crown Dancers among the Western Apaches. For the Jicarilla Apaches the young teenage boys are celebrated as they participate in the ceremonial relay races and as partners to the girls having their puberty feasts. Not all Apache children go through these types of ceremonies today, unless they still believe in the traditional ways.

Young Jicarilla men and boys are proud to be runners at ceremonial and annual relay races at Stone Lake. (Courtesy of Dina Velarde)

According to the U.S. Census Bureau's 2000 Census, 33.5 percent of the Apache population consisted of children under 18 years of age.[6] Children live in various households including those with two parents, those with single parents, and those with relatives and grandparents. Children also live in households with more than one family, or with a family that includes relatives and grandparents. By state laws, all children are to be in school from Head Start, from the ages of about 5 to 18 years of age.

In the general U.S. population, child care is provided primarily by day care centers. Grandparents have a limited role in child care as many of them are also employed, but according to the U.S Census Bureau's American Community Survey Report for 2004, 57.6 percent of American Indian and Alaska Native grandparents were responsible for co-resident grandchildren.[7]

TRADITIONAL CUISINE

When the Apaches were placed on their reservations, their traditional food and game resources, which were obtained from a wide and expansive area of lands, became limited or inaccessible. As reservation residents, these indigenous hunters and gatherers became recipients of government food rations consisting of wheat flour, salt, white sugar, baking powder, lard, coffee, and beef, if it was available. These rations were issued by the government Indian agent from the agency headquarters, which were usually located close to either a main road or railroad. The rationale behind the issuing of food staples was to provide assistance to the Indians during the transitional period from their hunting and gathering days to the time they became full-fledged farming communities. Each head of household was issued food rations, based on a census roll that listed the names of all the families, at least once a month by the government Indian agency. This meager foreign diet, consisting mainly of carbohydrates, was to replace the balanced and nutritious diet of the Apaches that consisted mostly of meat from wild game for their proteins and fat, and natural plant foods that included nuts and berries.

Indians were expected to become farmers raising livestock like cows, pigs, and chickens and to plant their own vegetables, like corn, wheat, potatoes, pumpkins, and squash. The problem with this government plan was it more caused suffering, starvation, and malnutrition than provided for the general welfare of the Indians. Beef contractors were not timely in their delivery, and suppliers and shippers were either late with their shipments and/or delivered inferior products and supplies. The Apaches were not totally helpless, since their vast reservation still provided wild game and plant foods, but in times of drought they had to rely on food rations.

The Western Apaches continued to collect mescal tubers, their food staple, in May. After the base portions of the plant, or crowns, and the leaves were shorn off, the mescal was roasted in large underground pit ovens. Cooked mescal was pounded into a coarse pulp, shaped into flat rectangular cakes, and again roasted in the ovens. Most of the roasted mescal was eaten on the spot, but a portion was dried in the sun and stored in ground caches for use as seed the following year.

In late June and early July, they gathered the fruit of the saguaro, prickly pear, and other cacti. Mesquite beans, the fruit of the Spanish bayonet and acorns of Emory's oak were collected in July and August. During the fall the men hunted deer and antelope, while the women and children gathered piñon nuts and juniper berries. Any meat was made into jerky.[8]

Money was needed to purchase farm animals and livestock, and the majority of the Apaches did not have jobs or any opportunities to earn money. As the most fertile lands had been taken by non-Indians, the marginal farming lands were all that were left to the Indians. Apache men viewed farming and gardening as women's work and initially refused to do it. While cows were acceptable and desired, chickens and pigs never went over very well with Apaches.

Farming was not a raving success on the Apache reservations but, eventually, with the help of the agency farmers, Apaches began to plant fields of corn, wheat, potatoes, and other hardy vegetables that could grow in high altitudes with short growing seasons, and oats, hay, and alfalfa for their livestock. The Indian boarding schools taught the Apache males farming and animal husbandry, irrigation, fixing farm equipment, carpentry, and masonry, as part of their industrial programs to help the school operate. Females were taught to cook, sew, wash, knit, and keep a household, as well as to help with the domestic chores in running of the schools.

Sheep and cattle ranching were great successes on the Apache reservations. As early as the turn of the twentieth century, Apaches were raising sheep and cattle. The raising of livestock became their source of income and they were able to purchase a greater variety of foods and products. The diet of the Apache people consisted of the Western ranch style food of mainly meat, potatoes, biscuits, coffee, and an assortment of vegetables (but mostly corn, beans, squash, and pumpkins when in season). Another important influence on Apache diet was the Hispanic and Pueblo people. The Southwestern cuisine consisting of chili stew, tortillas, fry bread, pastries, and pinto beans became standard foods for Apaches.

Since confinement to reservations, several factors have impacted the cuisine of the Apache people. The hunting and gathering of food sources from over a range of several thousands of acres was limited to the reservation boundaries. The industrial revolution in the United States made food products available to everyone with the income and access to markets. The invention of the tin can, the packaging of food products, the use of preservatives, and the affordability of these products also impacted the Indians on reservations. The agency trading post and stores in nearby towns offered canned meat and vegetables, bread, pastries, snacks, candy, and soda, to mention a few. Indian people had access to these types of products and their purchase was only limited by the Indian people's income.

By the 1920s, raising livestock was a major means of producing income for many Indian families. Because cattlemen typically only sold their livestock once a year and shepherds twice a year, they developed a relationship for obtaining credit from the trading post trader or from merchants in nearby towns and villages to purchase goods, supplies, and groceries. The access to products like white flour, refined sugar, products with high sugar and salt content, and artificial preservatives changed the diets and cuisine of the Apache people. From the 1920s through the 1960s, income levels remained in the poverty levels and Apache people had to rely on their own resources for their food.

The traditional diet of the Apache people was healthy, nutritious, and delicious. The majority of the Apache people prior to the late 1960s lived in rural areas of their reservations, most of them from livestock families. This lifestyle provided them with much physical exercise. Living out on the reservations, their meat was obtained from their own herds of cattle, sheep, and goats. While farm animals like chickens, hogs, and pigs were a standard on U.S. farms, the Apache people did not favor these animals and many ranches did not raise them, though there were some Apache people who did raise them. The traditional Apaches had a dislike for pigs and hogs because these animals were not averse to occasionally eating snakes and insects. The eggs and bacon breakfast was not the typical food for Apache people.

In addition to their livestock, the hunting and fishing of wild game also provided meat for Apache families. On the larger Arizona and New Mexico Apache reservations, there was, and still is, sufficient land for deer, elk, wild turkeys, pheasant, and rabbits. Prior to the 1960s, hunting was permitted year round, but that changed and now tribal members have to obtain hunting and fishing licenses from the tribes. Fishing in the numerous lakes is also permitted with proper licenses. Historically, because of their religious views, traditional Apaches did not consider fish a proper food. Fish was considered a relative of the snake and, therefore, not to be eaten. Today, many Apaches do not subscribe to this point of view and fish is part of their diet.

The cuisine of the Apaches is generally defined by the period when Apache people were primarily livestock owners. The basic diet consists of meat, potatoes or pinto beans, bread, and coffee for all meals. Eating three times a day is a U.S. custom, but for many Apaches, a big meal at breakfast and dinner was the standard, usually around eight a.m. in the morning and late afternoon around five to six p.m., and a small lunch or snack at noon depending on the time and circumstances. This schedule was due to the type of work required by livestock people and the amount of food that was available. Often, a rancher was out on the range around noon and could not get back to the house for lunch. This schedule, like many aspects of life, changed to the more common three meals a day as Apaches moved away from the livestock industry toward a wage-earning economy and from rural ranches to tribal towns.

The meat, potato, and bread cuisine was varied only by the imagination of the cook. The meat either was fried, boiled, or dried. Diced beef, lamb, goat, deer, or elk meat, from more desirable cuts of legs, tenderloins, or breast, could be fried in lard with sliced red or white potatoes. If fresh corn, squash, pumpkins, and onions were in season or available as canned vegetables, they were added to the meat for a delicious succotash-meat dish. Spices, like onions and wild parsley, could be added. The vegetables could also be cooked separate from the meat. Fried ribs from beef, mutton, lamb, and deer or elk was cooked in a kitchen oven or on a wire rack on an open fire. Different cuts of the meat were also prepared as separate dishes. Some were fried, roasted, boiled, or dried. In the days when Apache people lived on ranches and did not have refrigeration and electric ovens, all parts of the animal, except the skins, horns, and hooves, were used for food. The tongue was boiled, the liver was fried, and the intestines were wrapped around pieces of fat and fried. The blood was put inside the stomach and boiled, and when it cooled it was served up like a gelatin type slice of pie. The head and feet of the animal, mostly from the cows and sheep, were either roasted or put into hot pits in the ground where a fire had been prepared . (The heads of the wild animals were usually returned to the woods as required by religious practices.) Coals from the fire kept the ground oven hot enough to roast the head and feet. When they were taken from the pit, the hair and skin fell off, leaving the meat succulent and ready to eat. Obviously, these parts of the animals had a very short "shelf" life, so they were prepared and eaten right after the animal was butchered.

Drying meat—mostly beef, mutton, deer, and elk—was a standard practice because Apache families did not have refrigeration and this was a practical method of storing the meat. The meat was cut into thin and almost "flat" pieces and hung on lines of wire similar to clotheslines, or on wooden racks or spread out on canvas or other cloth materials to dry in the sun. It took at least a week to dry the meat, and it was stored in dry cool places in cloth bags. This dry meat was used to make stews and soups, or fried with potatoes. It was also crumbled until it became almost flaky and was added to potatoes, both fried and boiled. It was also added to boiled rice for breakfast. It was eaten "raw" and made very handy snacks for children and adults. It was easy to carry and did not spoil for a long time.

A favorite method of cooking the meat was simply to roast it in the oven or on ashes on an open fire. Boiling the meat with potatoes and eating with tortillas, biscuits, or fry bread has become known as Apache stew. Often corn, squash, carrots, onions, or other vegetables and natural herbs could be added. This Apache stew has been the "national food" for Apache people. It is served at home, at feasts, at ceremonies, and all other social gatherings.

Almost no meal is served without bread. There are four major types of bread: tortillas, biscuits, yeast bread, and fry bread, all made from white flour, shortening (or lard), salt, and baking powder.[9] The difference in the breads is how they are prepared and cooked. Tortillas were adopted from the Hispanic people of the Southwest by the Apache people when the Spanish arrived in the Southwest. It is made from dough that is patted round and flat, about six inches in diameter and cooked either directly on top of an iron stovetop or on a square or round flat iron grill pan. It is usually cooked fresh for every meal. Biscuits are made into rolls and fried in bread pans in an oven. Yeast bread is also made like biscuits and cooked the same way.

In the ranching days, yeast bread was cooked in an outdoor oven. They were similar to the outdoor ovens of the Pueblo people, except they were not as large. The round-shaped oven was made from a stone and plastered with a special mortar mixed of sand and soil. A fire was built inside the oven and when it was nice and hot, the ashes were cleaned out and the floor of the oven was coated with a thin layer of lard to keep the dough from sticking to the floor. The ovens varied in size but the average one had a radius of about three feet, measured about six feet in diameter, and had a hole in it to let out the smoke. The bread was put into this oven using a large flat stick about the size of a broom. The smoke hole was closed up with damp burlap tied onto a stick. Up to 10 loaves of bread could be baked at one time, and it took less than an hour to cook the entire batch. When the bread was removed, butter or lard was put on the top to keep it moist. This type of bread was made for a feast or large gathering or simply when the cook wanted to serve it up as an alternative to tortillas and biscuits. This baking process was very time consuming and it is not practiced very widely today.

Fried bread is cooked in deep skillets filled with lard or shortening on the stovetop or on an open fire on a grill. The bread is prepared like a tortilla and put into a hot skillet until it is browned on both sides. It is best when it is hot, so it is prepared just before a meal.

Jicarilla woman making bread for family meal. (Courtesy of Dina Velarde)

Besides the standard fare, there are other Apache foods made from vegetables and berries. Roasted corn is a favorite. It is roasted in an oven or in the ashes of an open fire. Corn is also made into soup or can be added to meat. The Apache people have planted corn for hundreds of years. When the Spanish arrived in Jicarilla country, they noticed that the Apaches who lived in rancherias were planting corn, and the early U.S. settlers in the White Mountains of Arizona also saw that the Apaches at the current Fort Apache Reservation were planting crops, including corn, along the river valleys. Corn was easy to grow and became a standard food crop for the Apache farmers and ranchers. Fields of corn were planted every spring. They were harvested in the fall and what was not eaten or used for cooking was dried and stored in root cellars in burlap sacks. The dried corn was called *chico* and was cooked with meat to make a delicious stew.

Potatoes were also planted in huge fields and like corn were plentiful. Potatoes were stored in root cellars so they were available year around. If the potatoes ran out, it was easy enough to get more at the store. Eventually, potatoes were easier to purchase, and today are not grown except in a few gardens. Other garden crops that were grown were peas, green beans, beets, turnips, radishes, and sometimes cabbage. Vegetables like broccoli, asparagus, cauliflower, spinach, kale, carrots, tomatoes, and lettuce were not vegetables grown in Apache gardens because these plants did not grow well in the Southwest climate without artificial means for watering. Fruits like apples, oranges, peaches, apricots, and grapes were not grown as a rule, due to the climate, but were either traded for meat from Hispanic and Pueblo people who lived along the river valleys of Arizona and New Mexico, or purchased from the stores. With the exception of wild berries, fruit was not a part of the traditional Apache diet.

Apache women made seasonal trips to the nearby mountains, valleys, mesas, and plains to gather various edible and medicinal plants, plants used in religious ceremonies, herbs, teas, root tubers, and materials for basket making. All varieties of berries, like chokecherries and wild blueberries that were ready for picking in late summer, were harvested and eaten fresh or dried in the sun and stored for later use. Patties were made from the crushed berries and dried in the sun. It was considered a sweet treat. The piñon nut is a favorite of Apaches, young and old. It grows on the piñon tree every four to six years, depending on the weather. Piñons are handpicked, cleaned, roasted, and sometimes salted and eaten as a snack. It is said that one cannot be an Apache unless one likes piñons.

Today, the basic Apache diet still consists of the meat-potato-and-bread cuisine. Added on to the traditional meats are chicken, turkey, pork, and fish, all fresh and canned and all purchased from grocery stores. Fish is still not a regular part of Apache diet, although there are many Apache fishermen who catch all species of fish found in lakes, streams, and rivers of the Southwest. The potatoes are no longer just fried and boiled, they are now mashed, baked, made into casseroles, French fried, made into salads, and eaten as potato chips. Backups to potatoes are rice and pasta, from macaroni to spaghetti. Vegetables, including fresh, frozen, and canned varieties, are now on family dinner tables as single dishes. Salads are still lagging but can be found on some dinner tables. Breads and cereals of vast varieties are offered, the same as at any typical U.S. grocery store. Fresh apples, oranges, and pears seem to be the favorites, but other varieties, like peaches, apricots, and mixed fruit from cans are also eaten. Desserts have not been on the Apache diet until the recent past. Today, all types of pastries, including pies, cakes, cookies, cupcakes, doughnuts, and ice cream are found in Apache pantries and food cabinets. Snacks like potato chips, candy, soft drinks, popcorn, and salted nuts are some of the foods Apache people eat.

Milk and dairy products of all types now grace the tables of Apache people. The main beverages for adults are still coffee and tea, although there is a preference for coffee with milk and sugar or milk substitutes and saccharine. Other beverages include soft drinks, fruit drinks, Kool-Aid, orange and apple juice, hot chocolate, and milk. In short, the Apache diet and cuisine is the typical U.S. diet consisting of meat, fat, vegetables, and other forms of carbohydrates, based on the food pyramid recommended by the U.S. Department of Agriculture and professional nutritionists.

The variety and quality of the foods eaten by individual Apaches are related to the level of income of the families, the types of products carried by the local stores, and by the willingness and ability to travel to the bigger towns and cities to do grocery shopping. Children are served hot lunches at the school cafeterias and senior citizens are also served hot lunches at senior citizens centers, or lunches can be delivered to their homes.

The modern social customs of Apache people, especially among those that live on the reservations, are a combination of the social customs of the past and the present. Many of the traditional Apache customs were modified, altered, or adapted to modern times but the core societal values remain intact in many ways. The traditional customs have fallen out of favor, been ignored, rejected, or replaced with customs of the dominant society for practical reasons, economic circumstances, and as an expression and choice of being an American. The adoption and acceptance of American ways have had dire social consequences, but Apache people have always had ingenuity and the ability to adapt and survive, and in due time they will find their answers and will continue to be Apache.

Notes

1. For an in-depth study on the modern role of Apache grandmothers, see Kathleen S. Bahr, "The Strengths of Apache Grandmothers: Observations on Commitment, Culture, and Caretaking," *Journal of Comparative Family Studies* 25(2):233–248. For a historical account, see Ruth McDonald Boyer and Narcissus Duffy Gayton, *Apache Mothers and Daughters: Four Generations of a Family* (Norman: University of Oklahoma Press, 1992).

2. Table 1b. Arizona American Indian Gender and Age Breakdowns by Reservation: 2000 from U.S. Census Bureau: 2000 Census, Table 15.

3. U.S. Census Bureau, 2004 American Community Survey, Selected Population Profiles, "Figure 2. Responsibility for Grandchildren Under 18 Years: 2004," *The American Community—American Indians and Alaska Natives: 2004*, 11.

4. U.S. Census Bureau, American FactFinder, Quick Tables, "DP—1. Profile of General Demographic Characteristics: 2000, Apache Alone (A09-A-23)," http://www.factfinder.census.gov (accessed April 1, 2010).

5. U.S. Census Bureau, 2004 American Community Survey, Selected Population Profiles, "Figure 4. Martial Status: 2004," *The American Community—American Indians and Alaska Natives: 2004*, 8.

6. U.S. Census Bureau, "Figure 1. Selected Age Groups and Median Age: 2000," *We the People: American Indians and Alaska Natives in the United States*, Census 2000 Special Reports (U. S. Department of Commerce, February 2006).

7. U.S. Census Bureau, 2004 American Community Survey, Selected Population Profiles, "Figure 2. Responsibility for Grandchildren Under 18 Years: 2004," *The American Community—American Indians and Alaska Natives: 2004*, 11

8. Keith Basso, "Western Apache," in *Southwest*, vol. 10 of *Handbook of North American Indians*, volume ed. Alfonso Ortiz (Washington: Smithsonian Institution, 1983), 468–469.

9. For traditional Apache food and its preparation on the White Mountain Apache Reservation see: Sharma, Sangita, Xia Cao, Joel Gittelsohn, Becky Ethelbah, and Jean Anliker, "Nutritional Composition of Commonly Consumed Traditional Apache Foods in Arizona," *International Journal of Food Sciences and Nutrition* 59(1):1–10.

6

Tribal Governments and Economies

ALL EIGHT of the Apache tribal governments have a special trust relationship with the U.S. federal government that had its beginnings in the sixteenth century when Spain discovered the New World. Colonial powers recognized Indian tribes as sovereign nations and began signing Indian land cession treaties with them. Out of this recognition and practice, when the Apache tribes came under the jurisdiction of the United States in 1848, the federal government, by its trust relationship with the Apaches, began providing for their general welfare. In 1934 it passed the Indian Reorganization Act, which allowed the Apache tribes to establish tribal governments. Since 1934, the Apache tribes have developed mainly viable natural resource-based tribal economies that include the livestock and tribal-owned recreation and tourism industries, agriculture and forestry, as well as oil and gas, mining, retail businesses, and gaming. The tribes have made great strides in developing their modern economies and communities.[1]

THE ROLE OF SPANISH COLONIAL LAW ON INDIAN LAND RIGHTS AND OWNERSHIP

Flying the flag of Spain, Christopher Columbus and his crew landed on the island of Hispaniola in 1492. Spain proclaimed jurisdiction over all the discovered lands and took symbolic possession of the Americas.[2] To govern the colonies, Spain established the Council of the Indies in 1511. This body made laws for the administration of the newly discovered lands. One set of laws was known as the *Recopilacion de Leyes de los Reynos de las Indias*. These laws governed and identified the land rights of the Indians. A Jesuit theologian, Francisco de Vitoria, was asked by Spanish king Charles V in 1532 to comment on the rights of the Indians in the conquered lands. De Vitoria declared that the Indian people were the true owners of the land and that discovery did not convey title of the land to Spain. Spain could not claim title under the rule of the divine right of the king or the pope. Only the voluntary consent of the Indians would justify annexation of their lands. The Spanish laws also provided protection for the Indians. The discoverers were not to carry out war against the Indians or do damage to them while trading with them.

This law became a theoretical cornerstone in how all European nations dealt with Indian nations and tribes in the Americas. After Spain lost its colonies to Mexico in 1821, Mexico continued to recognize Spanish laws in governing Indian lands. The legal principle that Indians were the true owners of the land and that it could not be taken without their consent eventually made its way into U.S. law and still stands today. It also became the basis for the relationship between the United States and Indian nations and tribes. To take possession of Indian lands, the Congress of the United States had to enter into a treaty, recognized as international law, with Indian tribes. During colonial times, Great Britain and France also entered into land and peace treaties with the Indian nations of North America. The practice was continued by the U.S. Continental Congress and, eventually, the United States since 1789.

INDIAN TRIBES AND THE U.S. CONSTITUTION

Indian tribes are the only minority group in the United States that are specifically mentioned in the U.S. Constitution, thus giving them a special legal status. Article I, Section 8, Clause 3 of the U.S. Constitution states that only the United States Congress can conduct commerce (trade) with Indian tribes. This provision reinforces the concept that Indian nations and tribes are quasi-sovereign nations and that only Congress has the power to deal directly with them. Indian tribes retain all rights to their lands and natural resources, as well as the right to govern themselves. For this reason, the U.S. states, like the states of New Mexico and Arizona, do not have full jurisdiction on Indian reservations.

INDIAN TRIBES AND THEIR POWERS OF SELF-GOVERNMENT

Indian tribes and nations, similar to individual states, retained certain powers of self-government. Indian tribes deal directly with the federal government on matters such as land, natural resources, education, and economic and technical assistance. It is because of the trustee relationship between the federal government and tribes that many tribes are not subject to certain state government laws and regulations.

ESTABLISHMENT OF APACHE TRIBAL GOVERNMENTS

All Arizona and New Mexico Apache tribes took advantage of the provisions of the Indian Reorganization Act (IRA) passed by Congress on June 4, 1934. By adopting this act, the Apache tribes established new forms of tribal governments that put them on the road to social and economic development. The purposes of the IRA were to improve Indian tribes' economic conditions by protecting their remaining reservation lands through conservation; to enlarge reservations through a land purchase program; to increase tribal members' political participation through self-government; and to encourage the preservation of tribal cultural heritage and tribal values.

The IRA required that elections be held in which all tribal members 21 years of age be allowed to vote on a tribal constitution and bylaws. These governing documents then had to be approved by the U.S. Secretary of the Interior. By 1938, all Arizona and New Mexico Apache tribes had their constitutions and bylaws approved. Under the tribal constitutions, all members were granted equal rights to life, liberty, industrial pursuits, and the economic resources of the tribe. No person could be denied the right to worship as he or she pleased, or the right to express his or her opinions, to assemble with others, or to petition for the redress of grievances. These same rights are also guaranteed to all citizens under the U.S. Constitution.

The new constitutions provided for representative tribal councils consisting of members who had to be at least 28 years old and residents of the voting districts on the reservations. Once a council was seated, it could elect an executive committee, a chairman, and a vice-chairman. The council met twice a year at the tribal headquarters. The members who received the largest number of votes served for four years and the others for two years. Elections were held every two years.

The first tribal councils were truly representative of the Apache people. The average age of a councilman was about 50 years old. These tribal elders were greatly respected by their people; most were spiritual leaders of the tribe as well as traditional political leaders of their communities. By electing these men, the Apaches were ensuring that their traditional values, ideals, and customs were protected within the framework of the modern constitutional government. In this way, continuity with the past was preserved as it adapted to modern political change.

The powers of this council were designed to protect and conserve the tribe's natural resources, to pass codes and regulations for the management of reservation lands for the benefit of the entire tribe, and to expend funds for its governmental operations and for the good of the tribe. Specifically, it had power to extend assistance to the needy, especially the elderly, as well as the power to preserve peace and order.

All the powers of the tribal governments reflected the traditional values of the Apache people. The protection, preservation, and conservation of the bounty of "Mother Earth," and all its inhabitants is a sacred value shared by all Indian people, and the Apaches were most eager to have this concept incorporated into their tribal constitution. Sharing with others is another basic idea that Indian people hold dear, and for this reason, the Apache constitutions stated that all the reservation lands were to be held for the benefit of the entire tribe. The creation of the tribal government was only the beginning for the modern Apache tribes. In many ways, the Apache constitutions reflected the spirit of the IRA, as well as the traditional values of the Apache people.

One of the provisions of the IRA was the establishment of the Revolving Credit Fund. The Apache tribal governments immediately began making important decisions that affected their lands and economies. For example, one of the first major decisions made by Jicarilla Apache Tribal Council was the return of all allotted lands to full tribal ownership. The wisdom of the elders was recognizable in this action. Although the northern part of the reservation was allotted under the General Allotment Act of 1887, most families had not received titles (known as land patents) by 1937. Despite the allotments, the Jicarillas had continued to share all of their lands for the raising of sheep and cattle, which required large amounts of pasturage. No surplus Jicarilla reservation lands were returned to the public domain or opened to settlement. The Jicarilla Apache Reservation is one of two reservations in the entire United States that is owned by the entire tribe and not individuals. This was the Apache way.

Under this new federal legislation, the Apache tribes soon improved their economies. Not only were all lands returned to tribal ownership, but a tribal corporation was created to manage the business of the tribe. Business loans were made to tribal corporations and to tribal governments to help purchase livestock herds. The San Carlos, Mescalero, White Mountain, and Jicarilla Apache tribes started very successful livestock operations and associations that became the foundations for economic progress. The revolving credit funds were used by the Apache tribes to support the tribes' livestock industries, tribal stores, and for the purchase of non-Indian land holdings within reservation boundaries.

By their greater participation in tribal affairs, through the creation of a tribal government, the Apache tribal members have steadily improved their overall living conditions. In the 1940s, the number of livestock increased on the reservation, and the natural result was an increase in personal income for Apache families. Like the U.S. government established by the Founding Fathers, the establishment of the Apache tribal government under the IRA not only reflected the ideals and principles of its society, but created a vehicle to face future changes.

THE ARIZONA APACHE TRIBAL GOVERNMENTS TODAY

Camp Verde Yavapai-Apache

The governing body for the tribe is an IRA nine-member community council consisting of a chairman, vice-chairman, and seven members, each serving staggered terms of four years. The tribes' constitution and bylaws were approved in 1937. They have both judicial and combination legislative and executive branches of government. The separate Indian communities of Camp Verde, Middle Verde, and Clarkdale combine to elect one council. In 1992, their name was formally changed to Yavapai-Apache Nation. The Camp Verde Yavapai-Apache Nation, under PL-638, contracts with the BIA to administer key programs and services. A complete list of tribal offices is as follows: administration, Apache culture, BIA police, community services, alcohol and substance abuse, higher education, social services, roads and maintenance, waste works, day care, economic development, enrollment, finance, fire station, housing, judicial, recreation, Clarkdale recreation, Middle Verde, seniors, and tribal police. In 2004, the administration was developing a security patrol for deployment in the housing department's neighborhoods. In 2004, the tribal council approved a judicial code. Drafts of the criminal code, the criminal rules of procedure, and the juvenile code were completed in 2003 and were to be approved by the tribal council in 2004.

San Carlos Apache

The tribal government, formed as a result of the IRA, is governed by an elected council representing four districts that operate under a written charter (ratified in 1955) and a constitution (adopted in 1936, revised in 1954, and amended in 1984). The council has a chairman, vice-chairman, secretary, and nine elected district representatives, each representing one of four districts. All serve staggered four-year terms. The Bylas district elects three council members, while Gilson Wash, Peridot, and Seven Mile districts elect two members each. The tribe, under PL-638, contracts with the BIA to administer key programs and services, such as the tribal court system, which includes tribal judges and the San Carlos Tribal Police Department, to enforce ordinances. Additional tribal departments manage the community's economic, educational, legal, health, and cultural affairs.

Tonto Apache

The tribal council, composed of a chairperson, vice-chairperson, and three other members, provides legislative authority and policy direction for all tribal programs. The chairman serves a four-year term, and the council members serve two-year terms. The tribe has seven departments: health and welfare, recreation, finance, personnel, contracts and grants, procurement, and maintenance. The tribe also has its own judicial system consisting of one judge, a court clerk, and an administrator. A tribal police department was established in 2002, and today there are seven officers and one chief of police; all are Bureau of Indian Affairs (BIA) certified. The Tonto Apache Reservation, under PL-638, contracts with the BIA to administer key programs and services, such as social services, the tribal court, roads, utilities, and law enforcement. The tribe funds its own higher education and vocational scholarships. Tribal government employs about 75 people, both Indian and non-Indian.

White Mountain Apache

The White Mountain Apache Tribal Council was established under the provisions of the IRA, adopting a constitution in August 1938. This constitution was amended in 1958 and 1993. The elected council includes a chairperson, who presides over all tribal council meetings and exercises authority delegated by law, ordinance, or tribal council; a vice-chairperson; and nine members at large elected from four districts, each serving a four-year term. The tribe, under PL-638, contracts with the BIA to administer key programs and services. The tribal chairman supervises a tribal legal office. In this capacity, the chairman has responsibilities similar to those of a federal or state attorney general. Tribal government has made a plethora of social services available to community members, including: the Job Training Partnership Act, WIC, weatherization, a safety department, food distribution, and elderly services.

THE NEW MEXICO APACHE TRIBAL GOVERNMENTS TODAY

Jicarilla Apache

Since 1937, the Jicarilla Apache Tribal Government has continued to play a critical role in the governance of the reservation and its people, who numbered about 3,400 in 2001. In 2000, the Jicarilla Apache Tribe officially changed its name to the Jicarilla Apache Nation through its tribal ordinance approved by the Secretary of the Interior. In the many decades of its existence, the tribal government has played an integral role in tribal economic development as well as in bringing prosperity to northern New Mexico. The Jicarilla economy has expanded by developing its oil and gas resources, timber resources, livestock ranching, and tourism and recreation. The land base has also increased by almost one hundred thousand acres through the purchase of five adjoining ranches.

The tribal government has evolved into a true replica of the U.S. form of government. The Jicarilla Apaches adopted their original constitution and bylaws on August 4, 1937, under the terms of the IRA. This constitution was revised in 1968. The legislative branch is composed of a legislative council of eight members who serve staggered terms of four years. The executive branch consists of a president and vice president, who are also elected every four years by tribal members 18 years and over. The president appoints the secretary and treasurer. The judiciary branch consists of a tribal court with up to two judges appointed by the president and an appellate court consisting of three members of the legislative council, also appointed by the president.

Today, the Jicarilla Apache Tribal Government is the principal provider of fire, rescue, and police protection for an area that covers more than 1,000 square miles of northern New Mexico. The tribal government's various agencies also provide environmental protection, fish and wildlife management, regulation of scholarship services, assistance to the elderly, and virtually every other governmental activity or service. The Jicarilla Apache Tribe has preserved and protected the traditional values of its Apache society, providing continuity with the past. It has established a governmental foundation to promote and adapt to modern change in the ever-changing world.

The tribe funds and operates its law enforcement program and tribal court. The tribal court consists of a judge, two associate judges, several contract judges, a prosecutor, and three administrative clerks. The court has jurisdiction over reservation domestic, criminal, civil, and child welfare cases. The tribal council is the appellate court.

Mescalero Apache

The Mescalero Apache Tribal Council, composed of a president, a vice president, and eight at-large members, serves as the governing body for enrolled tribal members. Council members are elected to two-year terms, with elections occurring annually. The original constitution and bylaws of the Mescalero Apache Tribe were ratified on March 25, 1936, in accordance with the IRA. The tribe adopted a revision on December 18, 1964. Tribal law was consolidated and codified under the Mescalero Tribal Code, approved on January 13, 1984. Long-range planning is directed by the tribe's overall economic development plan, adopted September 8, 1961, and periodically amended under the direction of a tribal staff.

The tribe contracts numerous programs through the BIA. They include law enforcement, forestry, youth development, natural resources, and social services. The tribe also maintains a tribal court, a law and order office, a drug court, human services, resource management and protection, historic preservation, and conservation programs. The Mescalero Tribal Court exercises jurisdiction over crimes committed on the reservation. The tribal civil and penal laws guide the court.

THE OKLAHOMA APACHE TRIBAL GOVERNMENTS TODAY

Apache Tribe of Oklahoma

A business committee, composed of a chairman, a vice-chairman, a secretary-treasurer, and two members, serves as the tribe's elected governing body. Committee members serve two-year terms; elections are held every two years in March. The Apache Tribe of Oklahoma incorporated in 1972, adopting a constitution and bylaws in accordance with the IRA and the Oklahoma Indian Welfare Act of 1936. The tribe is a PL-638 self-governance tribe. Tribal programs include food distribution, elder care, a vocational rehabilitation center, Indian Child Welfare, child care services, elimination of violence against women, higher education, Head Start, environmental, tax commission, and a tribal court.

Fort Sill Apache

The tribe ratified a constitution and bylaws on October 30, 1976, which had been approved by the Commission of Indian Affairs on August 18, 1976. An official tribal membership roll was established in 1977. A committee, composed of a chairperson, a vice-chairperson, a secretary-treasurer, and three members, serves as the elected governing body. Elected members serve two-year, staggered terms, with elections occurring annually. Absentee voting allows out-of-state residents to play a part in the tribe's governing. On July 18, 1975, the tribe and the BIA agreed upon the conditions of a tribal government development plan, which provided for the establishment of a federally recognized form of government for the Fort Sill Apache Tribe. The tribe is a self-governance tribe. Departments and programs existing within the tribal government include housing, accounting, a community health program, a language program, an emergency youth shelter, a nutrition program for aging tribe members, and an energy office.

MODERN APACHE TRIBAL ECONOMIES

The Forestry Industry

The Apache tribes are intent on managing their resources in the best possible manner in order to secure a productive land base for future generations while sensibly preserving the delicate ecosystem of tribal lands. The largest acreage of forestlands is on the Fort Apache Reservation at about 800,000 acres, followed by about 400,000 acres at San Carlos and about 400,000 acres on the Jicarilla Apache Reservation. The Mescalero Apache Tribe has about 175,000 acres. The Fort Apache Timber Company owned by the White Mountain Apache Tribe manages the tribe's forestry program. The Mescalero Forest Products is in charge of the forest industry on that reservation.

Today, the Apache tribes of Arizona and New Mexico collectively have over 1.5 million acres of forest and woodlands that contribute to their tribal economies. The forests consist primarily of ponderosa and piñon pine, spruce, fir trees, juniper, and oak. Ponderosa pine represents the majority of commercial tree species. Several of the Apache timber companies operate large facilities consisting of sawmills, planning mills with dry kilns, and operating budgets of over $5 million annually. The forests are managed to secure sustainable production of forest products. The saw timber is harvested under strict controls so as to maintain a tree canopy of many age classes. Between 1992 and 2002, over 74 million board feet was cut from just the Jicarilla Apache Reservation forestlands. Mescalero Forest Products and the BIA forestry branch jointly harvest approximately 20 million board feet of timber annually.

Finished Lumber at the Fort Apache Lumber Company, Whiteriver, Arizona. (Courtesy of Tiller Research, Inc)

The tribes have been very active in preserving and restoring natural resources on tribal lands for a number of years. Projects include reintroducing wildlife, improving and restoring wildlife habitats, and excellently managing all wildlife resources. The tribes practice comprehensive forest management, including prescribed burn, development backlog, and reforestation methods.[3]

The Livestock Industry

It was the goal of the federal government to make farmers out of the Apache people in the late 1880s when they were finally settled on their reservations, but the Apaches preferred raising livestock. The livestock industry was introduced to the various Apache reservations at different times between the late 1800s and the 1920s. After the turn of the twentieth century, Fort Apache residents began to enter the wage economy, including the U.S. Cavalry, working primarily as cowboys and hands on ranches and at the fort. Due to their growing population, in 1918 the federal government issued 400 cattle to the Apaches so that they might develop their own livestock industry.

It was not until the 1920s that livestock was introduced on the Jicarilla Apache Reservation. The livestock industry was a thriving economic force on this reservation through the early 1960s. Not surprisingly, it was the recognition of the feasibility of the timber industry that gave rise to livestock. When the government finally allowed the sale of timber between 1910 and 1922, the timber revenue was used to purchase sheep for the Jicarilla people. Later, many Jicarillas chose to raise cattle instead of sheep. The livestock industry has been the primary use of reservation land since 1890. Today, ranching serves as the primary agricultural enterprise on the Jicarilla Apache Reservation and features many family-operated cow-calf operations. The raising of sheep dominated this industry until 1960 when cattle raising increased. Ranching constitutes the sole private business sector on the Jicarilla reservation.

Tribal cattle raising was introduced on the San Carlos Reservation in 1923 by the BIA superintendent. In 1963, the San Carlos tribal government passed an ordinance that eliminated the BIA from the management of the tribal cattle herds. In the late 1980s the San Carlos cattle herd was estimated at 15,000, creating full-time to seasonal employment for about 200 people. The gross revenue from cattle sales was approximately $2.8 million.[4]

The livestock ranching was the only feasible industry on all the Apache reservations until about the 1950s when, due to market conditions, drought, and the high cost of operations, the Mescalero, San Carlos, and White Mountain Apache tribal governments decided to establish cattle raising as tribally owned enterprises. The Jicarilla Apache Tribe did not start a tribally

Everett Serafin and Bob C. Velarde branding cattle at the Velarde Ranch near Lindrith, New Mexico. (Courtesy of Matthew Rougé)

owned cattle herd until the 1960s. To support their cattle industry, cattle associations were established to manage the herds. In 1988 the San Carlos cattle industry was based on five independent ranch associations and two tribally managed ranches.[5] Today, the White Mountain Apache Tribe has a 15,000-head tribal herd, primarily consisting of purebred white-face cattle, generating up to 50 or more full-time jobs. As support for the cattle industry, the tribe runs a feedlot, a hay-and-grain store, and a 900-acre irrigated farm that produces alfalfa for feed.

San Carlos's cattle ranching operations are its third-largest source of income, generating over $1 million in annual livestock sales. Five tribal cattle associations (each with its own board of directors) manage the industry for the reservation, raising commercial Hereford cattle as well as tribally owned herds.

THE AGRICULTURAL SECTOR OF THE APACHE RESERVATION ECONOMIES

On the Jicarilla Reservation there are approximately 58,000 acres of irrigable land; currently only 6,496 acres of dry farming land and 1,000 acres of irrigated land are in use. The 1990 crop production was valued at $365,000. In the mid-1990s, the tribe acquired the Willow Creek Ranch, which has since been developed as a tribal enterprise. The site includes a

1,000-acre irrigation project and it is utilized as an agricultural career development, training, and research center. It was a joint effort involving the tribe, New Mexico State University, the U.S. Department of Agriculture, and the BIA Branch of Natural Resources.

San Carlos Tribe considers the redevelopment of agriculture a high priority. Reservation farms have generated profit from crops such as alfalfa and jojoba beans. With assistance from the BIA, the tribe revamped its extensive irrigation facilities by installing new pipelines and irrigation pumps, and by reconditioning ditches. An agricultural development committee oversees the future of the reservation's agricultural lands. Soil erosion and contamination is closely monitored on the reservation.

The Camp Verde Yavapai-Apache Tribe leases 180 acres of reservation land to non-Indians for farming, which generates an annual income; 180 acres are leased for irrigated agriculture; and there are beef and dairy cattle on another 180 acres of reservation rangelands. The herds, poultry, and irrigated crops of hay, grain, and fruit provide income for tribal members. Tribal lands that have been mined for sand and rock, then been reclaimed, are subsequently utilized for planting.

The Fort Sill Apache Tribe and the Apache Tribe of Oklahoma lease their lands to non-Indians for cattle grazing and agriculture, although the tribes and individual tribal members also farm and ranch their lands.

THE APACHE TRIBAL RECREATION AND TOURISM INDUSTRIES

The foundation of Apache life, including the reservation economy, has always been the natural environment and natural resources. The natural resources on all the Apache reservations have become the catalyst for their modern-day economies, consisting mainly of outdoor recreation, tourism, wildlife programs, and gaming. On all the Arizona and New Mexico Apache reservations there are mountains, valleys, deserts, rivers, lakes, streams, canyons, plains, and a wide range of wildlife and plants that have provided economic development opportunities. Outdoor recreation consisting of hunting, fishing, hiking, camping, swimming, skiing, canoeing, rafting, boating, kayaking, rock climbing, horseback riding, and outdoor adventures of all types are available on all Apache reservations.

Despite the abundance of natural resources and their scenic and economic value, the Apache tribes did not always see tourism as an economic development opportunity. It was not until the 1960s through the Johnson administration's War on Poverty programs, especially under the Office of Economic Opportunity, that tourism was developed on the Apache reservations. As result there was a tenfold increase in federal funding for economic development that seemed to center on tourism, particularly the building of hotels. The War on Poverty program was a response to the high unemployment rate on Indian reservations.

Today, the Apache reservation outdoor recreation and wildlife programs are some of the best in the United States. White Mountain Apache Tribe Wildlife and Outdoor Division activities include a hunting program, a rent-a-lake program, river running, and canyoneering. Fishing, hunting, backcountry safaris and tours, and other outdoor adventures are huge tourist attractions. There are innumerable wildlife viewing opportunities along 800 miles of streams and 30 artificial lakes and reservoirs covering 2,300 acres to provide a wide variety of fishing and camping experiences. Visitors can enjoy year-round trout fishing, winter ice fishing, and a number of tribally operated campgrounds. Mountain biking, swimming, horseback riding, rock climbing, rappelling, canyoneering, and wilderness hikes are also very popular activities on the reservation. Whitewater rafting, canoeing, and kayaking are possible on the Salt River, which originates on reservation lands.

The rich and diverse ecosystems of the Sonoran Desert provide numerous activities on the San Carlos Reservation. Hunting, fishing, camping, and recreation fees provide income to the tribe. Hunting for big and small game (such as elk, bighorn sheep, antelope, javelina, wild turkeys, and migratory birds) is available year-round. There are also opportunities for whitewater rafting, kayaking, and canoeing in the Salt River Canyon and charted hiking and camping trails throughout tribal lands. San Carlos Lake, formed by the construction of Coolidge Dam on the Gila River, is the largest body of water in the state, offering 158 miles of shoreline and stores 19,500 acres of water. It is full of largemouth bass, catfish, crappie, and sunfish. Talkalai Lake is another warm-water fishery on the reservation. It is stocked with trout, bass, channel catfish, crappie, and bluegill. San Carlos Lake Development Corporation, a tribal entity, has significantly improved lakeside campgrounds by remodeling the ramadas and installing a concrete boat ramp at Soda Canyon. There are also a remodeled store and tackle shop, a boat storage facility, and a RV and mobile-home park.

U.S. Highway 60, a direct route between Globe and Show Low, Arizona, in the north, cuts through the Salt River Canyon, commonly called the Mini Grand Canyon. During the spring melt-off in the higher elevations, this river runs fast and deep and hosts the popular sports of whitewater rafting, kayaking, and canoeing. The reservation is within 50 miles of the southeast border of Tonto National Forest and within 25 miles of the designated wilderness areas of Superstition and Salt River Canyon, which increases tourist traffic to the reservation. Other popular fishing destinations are Point of Pines Lake, a high mountain lake; Seneca Lake, just north of Globe; and the Black River and Salt River recreation areas, at the reservation's northern border.

JICARILLA APACHE TOURISM AND RECREATION

The Jicarilla Apache Reservation is located in a major regional, growing, multi-season recreation and tourism zone. Within its boundaries are 15 mountain lakes and vast wilderness areas. The reservation provides numerous outdoor activities, including hunting, fishing, sightseeing, and lake and river sports. Camping and picnicking are permitted around the reservation lakes where picnic tables, grills, and shelters are available. Many visitors also enjoy hiking, exploring, and taking trail rides through the reservation.

The tribe owns the Lodge at Chama, a 32,000-acre ranch situated in the San Juan Mountains. Visits to the lodge include access to recreational opportunities such as fishing, hunting, hiking, horseback riding, snowshoeing, skiing, snowmobiling, wildlife touring, and winter sleigh riding. Guests may also observe day-to-day ranch operations.

MESCALERO APACHE TOURISM AND RECREATION

In addition to the Inn of the Mountain Gods Resort and Casino and other tribal gaming facilities, the Mescalero Apache Tribe offers several attractions that appeal to visitors. The tribe operates the Silver Lake, Eagle Creek, and Ruidoso recreation areas. Silver Creek, located at the southern end of the reservation along State Route 244, and Eagle Creek, located at the northern end of the reservation along the ski road, offer full RV hookups, tent sites, picnic areas, and fishing. Ruidoso recreation area, located west of Ruidoso in the Upper Canyon region, offers tent sites, picnic areas, and fishing.

The tribe also owns the Ski Apache Resort. Ski Apache is southern New Mexico's premier ski area, with high-speed quad chairs and the state's only gondola. Located in the Sacramento Mountains, Ski Apache opened in 1961. It offers guests a certified ski school for all abilities, ski and snowboard rentals, round-trip scenic rides for non-skiers, and the Kiddie Korral for small children.

OTHER APACHE TOURISM AND RECREATION

The smaller Arizona Apache tribes—the Tonto Apache and Camp Verde—do not have the benefit of vast tribal lands but they do benefit from their locations near state recreational areas, as well as their own recreational activities. The Camp Verde Indian Reservation lies within the Coconino National Forest. The Montezuma Well and Tuzigoot prehistoric Indian Prescott National Forest lies to the east and the Kaibab National Forest to the north. Tonto National Forest is also nearby. Fort Verde State Park, where four of the original adobe buildings stand open to the public, is located nearby in the town of Camp Verde. The park's museum contains early military artifacts, Indian relics, and implements used by the earliest Verde Valley settlers. Three area national monuments—Montezuma Castle, cliff dwellings, and pueblos—are within 25 miles of the reservation.

Ideally situated to take advantage of the high volume of tourism in and around the Payson area, the Tonto Apache Reservation adjoins the Tonto National Forest, an area rich with outdoor recreation opportunities, including hunting, camping, and winter sports such as skiing, cross-country snowshoe racing, and snowmobiling. The reservation is just minutes away from the scenic Mogollon Rim, a steep escarpment dividing Arizona's northern plateau region from the lower desert areas in south-central Arizona. Other local attractions include a fish hatchery and Tonto Natural Bridge, the largest travertine bridge in the world.

White Mountain Tribe owns and operates one of the region's best ski resorts, the Sunrise Park Ski Resort. Sunrise Park Ski Resort, the largest in Arizona, offers downhill skiing with 65 runs for skiers at all levels of proficiency, a separate snowboarding area, and cross-country ski trails.

In Oklahoma, the Apache Tribe of Oklahoma is near the Wichita Mountains 30 miles southwest of Anadarko, providing an abundance of outdoor recreational activities.

Jicarilla Apache Fisheries

Harvard University's Honoring Nations program recognized the Jicarilla Tribe's wildlife and fisheries program in 1999. The program is one of the largest and most respected fish and wildlife management initiatives on the continent. It manages a 14,500-acre game park and has implemented a number of projects that preserve the wildlife population and, at the same time, create a significant source of revenue for the tribe. The fish stock in tribal waters include rainbow, brook, brown, and cutthroat trout; bluehead sucker, flannelmouth sucker, speckled dace, and mottled sculpin. Reservation lakes are restocked annually with about 100,000 fish, and the larger lakes are managed as "put, grow, and take" sites. Annual gill netting surveys are conducted at the lakes, and populations are monitored closely.

Mescalero Apache Fisheries

In 1999 the tribal hatchery was closed by the U.S. Fish and Wildlife Service due to damages caused by fires and flooding. Since that time, the Mescalero Apache Tribe has assumed control of the facility. In 2004, functions were restored and the cultivation of the rainbow trout resumed. Plans for renovation include updating equipment in order to increase production. The tribe also plans to initiate propagation of the Rio Grande cutthroat trout. The tribe is a member of the Southwest Tribal Fisheries Commission.

THE RETAIL AND SERVICES SECTOR OF THE APACHE RESERVATION ECONOMIES

All the Apache tribes own and operate retail outlets and offer various retail services. The retail stores include grocery stores, convenient marts, restaurants, gas service stations, gift shops, lumber stores, RV parks, and banks.

THE MINING SECTOR ON THE APACHE RESERVATIONS

Deposits of peridot in Arizona are the major U.S. source of the semiprecious gemstone. Peridot is found only in the Red Sea, in Myanmar (formerly Burma), and on the San Carlos Apache Reservation. The yellow- to olive-green gem is highly prized for the manufacture of birthstones and other jewelry. It is estimated that 80 to 95 percent of the world's supply of peridot is mined on basalt-lined Peridot Mesa at the reservation, making it the single largest productive peridot mine in the world. Once sold primarily in lots of uncut material, in 2004 many individuals were contracting for cutting services and marketing the cut stones.

The Camp Verde Yavapai-Apache Tribe owns a sand and gravel mining operation. It owns 30 percent interest in Drake Cement, a Peruvian-based cement manufacturing plant owned by ARPL. The tribe is working with owners to build a sister-operation in Drake, Arizona. Construction of the plant was to have to begun in 2005.

Located in the San Juan Basin, the Jicarilla Apache Reservation contains the second-largest gas field in the continental United States. The region produces more oil than any basin in the Rocky Mountains. Its resources include large amounts of oil, gas, coal, uranium, and geothermal reserves. Underneath the entire reservation are coal reserves, while oil and gas pools can be found under the southern portion of the reservation.

In 1977, the Jicarilla Apache Tribe became the first U.S. tribe to be the sole owner and operator of an oil and gas production company. Second only the federal government, the tribe is the largest mineral owner in the San Juan Basin. Over the past three decades more than 2,700 wells have been drilled. The tribe's mineral reserves serve as its largest source of revenue.

Natural resources found on Oklahoma tribal lands include an abundance of oil and gas. During the 1920s and 1930s, these resources were highly sought after. Rather than being required to deal directly with Native landowners, the state permitted mining companies to negotiate all leases and contracts with state agencies. In a number of cases, the landowners were actually children. In many of those cases, the state agent would sign leases on behalf of the child. Language barriers often prevented adult involvement in the negotiation process, and the state agent would intercede and negotiate the contract in those instances as well. Consequently, many tribal members were

Fred Vigil, JAECO Production Supervisor, reading meter run on Jicarilla Apache Reservation. (Courtesy of Bobbie Nell Vigil)

subject to agreements they had taken little or no part in. An overwhelming number of tribal members were defrauded, albeit legally, of the financial compensations they should have been entitled to. The Fort Sill Apache Tribe has since sought legal recourse, arguing that the state policy that allowed this activity violated the rights of tribal members and prohibited them from receiving the appropriate compensation for land leases. The tribe is now receiving royalties from their oil and gas leases.

THE INDIAN GAMING INDUSTRY ON THE APACHE RESERVATIONS

The industry of gaming began with the passage of the federal Indian Gaming Regulatory Act of 1988. Under this act, all federally recognized Indian tribes were eligible to start gaming operations on their reservations. The purposes of the act are to generate revenue for the tribes and to promote tribal economic development, self-sufficiency, and strong tribal governments. After Indian tribes enter into state compacts, they can set up casino and other gaming enterprises. All the Apaches tribes of Arizona, New Mexico, and Oklahoma have taken advantage of the act and started gaming operations on their reservations.

APACHE INDIAN GAMING IN ARIZONA

The Yavapai-Apache Tribe of Camp Verde

The Yavapai-Apache opened the Cliff Castle Casino in May 1995 on 72 acres adjacent to Montezuma Castle National Monument. The casino has become a major private employer for the reservation, with over 300 employees in the year 2000. The casino complex features a restaurant, a bowling center, a malt shop, and a play area for children. Live entertainment at the facility includes comedians, bands, dancing, karaoke, televised sporting events, and an open-air venue, the Stargazer Pavilion, where concerts, pow-wows, professional wrestling, and bike rallies are held.

Revenues generated by gaming have enabled the Nation to (1) raise the entire community's standard of living; (2) supply additional social services to the elderly; (3) provide educational opportunities for all ages; (4) serve as the foundation for growing the Nation's land base; (5) foster long-term economic development; and (6) fund tribal programs to nurture and support traditional customs and values.

The Yavapai-Apache Nation believes in sharing its good fortune with its non-Indian neighbors. Every year since 2000, it has awarded college scholarships to three non-Indian graduating seniors, one from each of the Verde Valley high schools. This scholarship program seeks to promote higher education and build bridges between the Yavapai-Apache Tribe and the greater community.

In 2006 the Yavapai-Apache Nation contributed more than $170,000 to support a wide variety of projects, including infrastructure in Camp Verde, athletic programs in the Clarkdale-Jerome schools, public safety in Sedona, and the remodeling of the Yavapai County Senior Center. It also supported a fire safety program for children through the Gilbert Fire Department.

San Carlos Gaming

The San Carlos Apache Tribe owns and operates the Apache Gold Casino and the Best Western Apache Gold Hotel, employing approximately 450 tribal members and non-members from adjacent communities. The resort complex includes convention space, a cabaret with nightly live entertainment, a gift shop, a RV park, a convenience store, two restaurants, and an 18-hole championship golf course. The Apache Gold Resort complex includes the Pavilion, a newly constructed, state-of-the-art, covered-roof multipurpose arena where rodeos, car shows, horse shows, concerts, and pow-wows are held.

Tonto Apache Gaming

In 1993, the Tonto Apache Tribe opened the Mazatzal Casino, which has a restaurant, a sports lounge, a gift shop, and an arcade. The casino is one of the major employers in the region, with over 300 employees, the majority of whom are non-Indians. Casino revenues generate much-needed financial support to tribal members for health, education, and better living conditions. Additionally, the tribe has donated several thousand dollars to various local nonprofit charities in Payson, Arizona, as well as to the school district. In 2006, it remodeled and expanded a recreation center and youth activities building in Payson. The facility included a nearly Olympic-sized swimming pool and a weight room as well as activity rooms for activities from traditional and electronic games to crafts and study materials.

The White Mountain Apache Tribe Gaming

This tribe operates the Hon-Dah Casino and Resort, a 15,000 square-foot facility that offers gaming, entertainment, and lodging for its guests. Hon-Dah is operated by Apache Enterprises, a tribally owned company that also operates the 130-room hotel and the nearby RV park. Hon-Dah is a major employer on the reservation.

APACHE INDIAN GAMING IN NEW MEXICO AND OKLAHOMA

Mescalero Apache Gaming

The tribe owns and operates the Inn of the Mountain Gods Resort and Casino just outside of Ruidoso, New Mexico. The resort offers a luxury hotel, a casino, a golf course, and banquet halls. The hotel features 273 luxury rooms and suites, 40,000 square feet of meeting space, an indoor pool, and a fitness center. The inn also features an 18-hole championship golf course that was rated one of the 35 best courses in the nation by *Golfweek* magazine.

Jicarilla Apache Gaming

In 2004 the Apache Nugget Casino opened its doors to business at the junction of State Highways 550 and 537. A small casino is also housed at the Jicarilla Inn in Dulce.

Apache Tribe of Oklahoma Gaming

The Apache Bingo Hall is located near the tribal headquarters. The tribe is considering expanding its gaming operation to include a casino.

Fort Sill Apache Gaming

The Fort Sill Apache Casino located in Lawton, Oklahoma, employs 100 people. As a corporate partner, the Fort Sill Apache Casino has become heavily involved in local community activities. The casino donated more than $10,000 in money and services in 2003 to support various charitable and tribal activities.

The large Apache tribes of Arizona and New Mexico share similar types of modern tribal governments that were organized under the IRA and established in the late 1930s. Their economies are based on their abundant natural resources and their sizeable land base. These lands have afforded them the opportunity to raise livestock that requires large amounts of grazing lands and to create an outdoor and recreation industry.

With the recent and increased funding from the federal government, the Apache tribes have taken advantage of entering into partnerships and cooperative agreements with their states and various federal agencies, which has allowed economic development. What has made this possible is the revenue from Indian gaming.

Notes

1. Portions of chapter 6 were previously published in Veronica E. Tiller, compiler, *Tiller's Guide to Indian Country: Economic Profiles of American Indian Reservations* (Albuquerque: BowArrow Publishing Company, 2005). Reprinted with permission.

2. Portions of chapter 6 were previously published in Veronica E. Tiller, "Native American Land and Water Rights Issues" in Semos Unlimited, *Nuevo Mexico: An Anthology of History* (Las Vegas: New Mexico Highlands University, 2009), 347–356. Reprinted with permission. Also see Robert J. Nordhaus, *Tipi Rings: A Chronicle of the Jicarilla Apache Land Claim* (Albuquerque: BowArrow Publishing Company, 1995), 3–5.

3. For in-depth studies on the forestry industry on two Apache reservations, see Arthur R. Gomez and Veronica E. Tiller, *Fort Apache Forestry, A History of Timber Management and Forest Protection on the Fort Apache Indian Reservation, 1870–1985* (Albuquerque: Tiller Research, Inc. 1990); see also Historical Research Associates, *The Mescalero Timber Trust: A History of Forest Management on the Mescalero Indian Reservation, New Mexico* (Missoula: Mountain Moving Press, 1981).

4. Jan Erik Hall, "Apache Cattle: The Reservation as Marketplace, a Sale Yard Feasibility Study," Harvard Project on American Indian Economic Development, John F. Kennedy School of Government, Harvard University, PRS 88-11, May 1988, 2.

5. Ibid. 2–3.

7

Contemporary Issues

THERE ARE A SERIES of contemporary social, economic, and cultural issues that have deep roots in the history of federal Indian policies that are of grave concern to the Apache tribes. These interrelated and intertwined contemporary issues go to the heart of the future survival of the Apaches as a distinct people and touches on their existence as Indian tribes. At the center of these issues is the concept of family. The question is whether Apache people will honor their cultural traditions with respect to restoring the family to its rightful position and role in their contemporary societies or allow the family unit to continue to erode in the face of modern times and circumstances. Tied to the traditional definition of family and tribal identities are the blood quantum requirements that identify who is and who is not an Apache, and who can or cannot be a tribal member. A related question is whether or not Apache tribes, as legal entities, will exist in the future if they rely on blood quantum to define tribal membership.

The breakdown of the family structure has had, and continues to have, dire consequences for Apache families and Apache tribes. The effects are clearly evident in the crime rate (especially the use of methamphetamine) and the suicide rates, as well the health issues surrounding and contributing to the high rates of obesity and diabetes among Apache people. The Apaches have come to a crossroad where they will have to make some critical decisions that will affect their future.

Survival, resiliency, and determination have been cornerstones in Apache character. These characteristics have brought the Apache people through hard times and have crowned their progress and achievements. Although faced with the erosion of the family structure, high rates of drug abuse, and endangerment of the language, among others, they have tackled their problems and have prevailed. Illustrations of their determination are their resolve to save their language, take on the problems of meth and suicide, and protect their environment. The most important trend has been the realization that Apache people are responsible for their future and that they have the means to be truly self-determined and to maintain the trust relationship with the federal government.

THE BREAKDOWN OF THE TRADITIONAL APACHE FAMILY AND ITS CONSEQUENCES

The importance of the family structure and its role in Apache society has diminished considerably in modern times. The traditional unit of Apache tribal societies has been the extended family, which consists of the nuclear family and close relatives, with women as the heads of household. The matriarchal family system was disrupted by the U.S. government's policies of assimilation, causing social problems that persist today. The adoption of the nuclear family, a dominant U.S. social institution, has caused disharmony and conflict among the Apache. On the one hand, Apache people still operate informally under the traditional ways with women as heads of household. Yet the modern system promotes men as the head of household. Aside from the socioeconomic structures outside the reservation boundaries, the idea of Apache men as head of household does not always work.

There are many reasons why the male head of household model cannot necessarily fit Apache lifestyles. One of the main reasons is economic. The federal government provides the bulk of economic development on Indian reservations while the tribe has control over all economic activity on Indian reservations. All federal funding goes directly to the tribe and the tribe is the major employer and owns all economic enterprises. With rare exceptions, there is no private business sector. The permanent jobs that exist are primarily in the areas of federal and tribal government and tribal enterprise management and administration. While these sectors employ a large number of people, it is still insufficient for full employment, thus unemployment rates remain high on all the Apache reservations.

Men are expected to be the head of household, which includes being the primary financial provider, but when there are limited jobs, there may be no source of income for them. Without a job, there are no unemployment benefits. Seeking employment off the reservation requires money, and perhaps higher qualification for jobs. Under these circumstances it is easier to remain on the reservation and compete for the temporary jobs or seek welfare assistance. Often, in these situations, if the woman in a household is employed, she becomes the "breadwinner" and, therefore, head of household.

There are numerous variations on the head of household concept that do not fit the patriarchal model, and reveal that it has not necessarily taken hold among Apache people. Statistics show a decrease in marriages in favor of single parenthood (and, consequently, women as heads of household), an increase in the number of single women heads of household, and grandparents as heads of households.

TRIBAL IDENTITY AND BLOOD QUANTUM REQUIREMENTS FOR TRIBAL MEMBERSHIP

Tribal identity and the concept of family are defined by blood quantum. This idea of blood quantum began as an economic measure by the federal government to fulfill its trust obligations in the early reservation era to feed the Apaches. Today, it governs who is and who is not recognized as an Apache by the tribe and the federal government. Blood quantum determines who can and cannot enroll as a tribal member.[1] It undermines the traditional notion of the Apache family and has the potential of legislating Apache people and Apache tribal governments out of existence in the next 50 years.

In the 2000 U.S. Census there were about 57,000 "full-blood" Apache people and there were 102,000 Apache people who claimed to be of mixed heritage. This trend in mixed heritage is expected to grow due to several factors. One is the small population size, especially for the four Apache tribes of New Mexico and Oklahoma. The small population creates a small "pool" of members who can marry each other without violating the rules of marrying close relatives. Moreover, the number of young Apaches leaving their reservations and communities to seek educational and employment opportunities in urban areas continues to grow. Often, they end up marrying non-Apaches. The growing numbers of intermarriages between Apache people and non-Apache people have a direct impact on Apache tribal identity and dire implications for the future for tribal membership, tribal enrollment requirements, and the future of Indian tribes.

Historically and traditionally, Apache tribal membership was simple. If a person had parents who were Apache, then he or she was an Apache. If an Apache person married a person from another tribe or a non-Indian, that non-Apache person became a member of the tribe, usually because the couple joined the family of the wife. If the couple chose to join another tribe and live away from Apache lands, the couple was still considered family and members of the Apache tribe. The children of this couple became members of the tribe and were given the same rights and privileges afforded all other members without regard to their non-Apache parent's lineage.

Often in the past, when there was famine, pestilence, or losses from wars, the Apache men raided other tribes to "replenish" the female population. The captives then became full members of the tribe. If other tribes captured Apache females, and if they returned to the tribe and brought children, the children were unconditionally accepted into the family of the returning female. The concept of family was that everyone who belonged to an Apache family was Apache.

The notion that tribal identity should be measured by blood quantum did not exist in the Apache tradition. It is a concept that originated during colonization in order to restrict people of indigenous heritage from rights that were intended for members of the dominant group. They were regarded, legally and socially, as inferior to whites and, therefore, not afforded the same rights. The character of people of mixed heritage, or "mixed-bloods," was measured by their indigenous heritage. In 1866, Virginia decreed that "every person not a colored person having one-fourth or more Indian blood shall be deemed an Indian."[2] Today this one-quarter blood is the standard used by the BIA and Indian tribes to determine who is an Indian and who is not. Blood quantum is seen as a product of white racism based on social science theories that aimed to prove the superiority of white people. In addition, the implementation of blood quantum requirements is also considered part of a plan to ensure that Native nations will vanish when the white blood quantum reaches a certain level (above three-fourths, for example).[3]

In the case of the Apache, the use of the blood quantum ranged from economic to political reasons. The original use by the federal government was to identify who was an Indian and who was not for purposes of providing food rations, supplies, and clothing by the Indian agencies when the Apache were first placed on reservations. Rations were given only to Indians who were on the ration or census rolls.

To qualify to be on a ration or census roll, an Indian person had to have more than one-quarter Indian blood. For Apaches this initially was not a problem because most Apaches were "full-bloods." As time progressed, many Apaches began intermarrying with non-Indians and Indians from other tribes. One reason was that the Apache had their cultural rules for marriages, that they could not marry close cousins on either side of their family. They understood that there were health and physical consequences for intermarriages, like susceptibility to diseases, physical disfigurement, and mental impairments. The Apache tribes with the smaller populations were especially cognizant of these consequences and encouraged intermarriage with non-Indians and Indians from other tribes. The problem with this was that it lowered the blood quantum of the offspring of those individuals who intermarried and placed them in a situation where they could be denied tribal membership, as well as their identity as Apache Indians. For example, if a Jicarilla Apache woman named Theresa married a San Carlos man named Joseph, their child, Sally, will be half-Jicarilla and half-San Carlos, though she is technically full-blooded Apache. Her parents have to select which tribe to enroll Sally in because, according to tribal rules of enrollment, an Indian person cannot have membership in two different tribes. Let's say they want to enroll her with the Jicarilla Apache Tribe. Sally is one-half Jicarilla. The blood quantum requirement for Jicarilla Apache tribal membership is three-eighths, therefore, Sally does qualify for membership.

But, in order for Sally's children to qualify for Jicarilla tribal membership and for them to retain their Apache identity (according to the existing blood quantum rules), the only choice for Sally is to marry a "full-blooded" Jicarilla Apache, or a Jicarilla Apache who has at least three-fourths Jicarilla blood. If she does not marry a Jicarilla man with these blood quantum requirements, her children will not qualify for tribal membership. However, if Sally's husband is a legally enrolled member of the Jicarilla Apache Tribe, and he does not meet the blood quantum requirements, they cannot enroll their children with the San Carlos Apache Tribe, despite the fact that the children are one-quarter San Carlos Apache. San Carlos requires that in order for a person to enroll with them, at least one parent has to be on their rolls. Although Sally's children meet the one-quarter blood quantum because Sally is half San Carlos, they cannot enroll at San Carlos. In effect Sally's children, who are full Apache, lose their legal Apache identity and rights to be tribal members due to blood quantum rules.

In effect, there is no freedom of choice in marriage partners if one wants to retain Apache tribal membership. Sally's grandchildren can regain their Apache blood quantum *only* if they marry other Apache people who are one-half or more Apache by blood quantum, but eventually the problem arises again for their children, especially if any of the marriage partners are non-Indian or from another tribe. This issue is critical in light of the fact that the number of Apaches of mixed heritage will increase in the future.

Apache tribes, which are quasi-sovereign governmental entities, have the sole power to determine their tribal membership requirements, but have selected to abide by the rules and policies of the federal government. The idea of blood quantum points to the eventual end of Indian people. In several more generations, the blood quantum requirements will have denied Apache people their tribal identities as well as their existence as tribal governments. The Apache tribes, who collectively own over 5 million acres of reservation lands, will witness the return of these lands to the public domain, as the Apache people who were denied tribal membership are forced to stand by and watch their ancestral homelands de-classified as tribal lands.

Historically, the main reason for adopting the blood quantum requirement was economic. The U.S. government did not want to be financially obligated or responsible to more Indian people, so the idea of blood quantum worked in their favor. The Apache people also knew that the more people were on their rolls, the less economic benefits they would receive from the federal government. In effect, the economic pie was not large enough to be divided with more Apache members. In addition, the Apache people did not (and maybe still do not) want "their blood" diluted with that of non-Indians and people from other tribes. While the blood quantum system may seem a viable solution to immediate economic problems, in the long run, the consequences are potentially tragic and the requirements go against the moral laws of the traditional concepts of Apache families. An obvious solution is to restore the traditional Apache definition as to who is an Apache.

THE IMPACT OF CRIME, DRUGS, AND ALCOHOL ABUSE

The breakdown of the family unit, as influenced by poverty due to limited jobs and high unemployment, has led to the rise of crime on the Apache reservations, especially crimes related to the use of methamphetamine. The increasing crime rate throughout all of Indian country has reached epidemic proportions in the last decade. The rate of violent criminal offenses in Indian country is 215.6 crimes per 100,000 inhabitants in non-metropolitan areas. The violent crime in Indian country is 101/1,000 inhabitants.[4] "American Indians experience one violent crime for every 10 residents over the age of 12 and the rate of violent crime victimization among Indians 25–34 was more than 2½ times the rate for all persons the same age."[5]

The rising crime is alarming and tragic, negatively impacting all Apache tribes, as well as all other tribes in the United States. The one single issue that has caused grave concern and immediate attention like no other is the use of the deadly drug methamphetamine, or meth, as it is commonly called. According to a 2006 National Congress of American Indians Report, in 2005 American Indians and Alaskan Natives had the some of the highest use rates at 1.7 percent. "This rate is substantially higher than other ethnicities: whites (0.7%), Hispanics (0.5%), Asians (0.2%) and African-Americans (0.1%). Reservation and rural native communities meth abuse rates have been seen as high as 30 percent."[6]

Tribal police forces ranked meth as the greatest drug threat to Indian communities and point to it as the cause in an increase in domestic violence and assault and battery. The FBI offices located in Indian country attributed meth in some capacity as the cause for 40 percent of violent crime on Indian country. It has been estimated "that 80–85 percent of the Indian families in child welfare systems have drug or alcohol abuse issues [and that the] recent increase in child related meth cases in Indian Country [was due to] child neglect rather than child abuse. . . . For example, the Yavapai-Apache Nation estimates that 90 percent of their open child welfare cases are related to methamphetamine."[7]

THE PROBLEM OF METHAMPHETAMINE ON THE SAN CARLOS APACHE RESERVATION

The Mexican drug cartel has targeted several reservation communities, especially those along the Arizona-U.S. border because they do not have the tribal or federal governmental social service infrastructure nor the consistent funding from the federal government for the social services required to fight the crisis created by the sale and use of meth. The San Carlos and White Mountain Apache Tribes have been hit hard by the drug trafficking due to the rural nature of their communities located over several million acres and their limited law enforcement resources.[8] As a relatively cheap stimulant, meth has found a niche in some Apache communities where poverty, depression, and substance abuse issues already exist.

Historically, there has been very little funding available for tribes from both the federal and state governments. Federal funding that is funneled through the states does not always find its way into tribal coffers, despite the fact that tribal members are counted in determining state allocations for federal monies. States are not required to share or allocate funds so, in many cases, the tribes addressing serious drug problems are forced to depend on an over-burdened and underfunded social service system.[9]

It was noted in 2006 that the rise and spread of meth use and its production on the San Carlos Apache Reservation was destroying the community by threatening the physical, cultural, and spiritual lives of the people. The most tragic effects of meth are those involving innocent children. It was reported that a 14-year-old meth user gave birth to an infant with a deformed pelvis and legs and no feet; another baby was born with congenital heart problems and still another child was born addicted to meth and with paralysis of the legs. A nine-year-old meth user was brought to the San Carlos Hospital with hallucinations and violent behavior. These are only a few of the tragic stories that illustrate the use of meth at San Carlos.

There were 101 suicide attempts directly related to the use of meth in 2004, with 2 resulting in death. Also in 2004, 64 babies out of 256 were born addicted to meth; 24 to 25 percent of pregnant women tested positive for meth. In 2005 the number of babies born to mothers addicted to meth remained high and resulted in birth defects, low birth weight, tremors, excessive crying, attention deficit disorder, and behavioral disorders. From 2004–2006 the San Carlos Hospital reported to the tribe's Child Protective Services a sharp increase in the treatment of meth-related ailments. About 80 percent of these cases involved alcohol or drug use. About 36 percent of reported cases of child neglect and abuse were repeated occurrences.[10]

The San Carlos Tribe's health care facilities, social services programs, and police department are overwhelmed by the meth problem, most of which is trafficked from Mexico. Related to meth and other drugs, there has been an increased gang and gun presence on the reservation, creating serious public safety problems. The police department lacks the manpower and equipment to investigate and make arrests for meth-related crimes. Over the past decade, it has experienced severe shortfalls in federal funding for law enforcement and social and health services. The police have been at a severe disadvantage in responding to all calls, with fewer than five officers to patrol nearly 1.8 million acres, and due to the time required to travel the long distances between the police districts.

Even with all the limitations, the San Carlos Police Department managed to deal with 20,590 offenses in 2004. In 2006 the San Carlos Apache Tribe took decisive action to prevent and eradicate meth from its reservation by coordinating with every tribal program and state and federal agency.[11] A Methamphetamine Prevention Coalition was formed to combat substance abuse and suicide. With the state of Arizona, the tribe launched an all-media meth awareness campaign to educate the community. The tribe implemented a meth outreach program for its employees and their families and a random drug testing policy for all its employees. Any employee who tested positive was terminated, referred to treatment, and required to be substance free for at least a year in order to requalify for tribal employment.

The tribe took swift and decisive action to alert meth dealers and their customers that the presence of meth on the reservation would no longer be tolerated. The San Carlos Law Enforcement was armed with a new legal code to enforce the anti-meth campaign, with stiffer penalties for violators. The state of Arizona and the tribe announced a policy of zero tolerance for all drug dealers, especially when it involved the victimization of children or the dealing on or near school grounds. Efforts were made to deal with the selling of meth to tribal members, certifying officers who are meth lab detection specialists, and educating San Carlos youth to make them aware of the deadly ramifications of meth.

The tribe, in partnership with the BIA and the state of Arizona, was successful in getting several convictions or guilty pleas of individuals dealing meth on the reservation. It is clear that the San Carlos Tribe is working to protect its communities against the deadly effects of meth and to safeguard the welfare of its people.

The Suicide Rate on the White Mountain Apache Reservation

Just as the use of meth is devastating the San Carlos Reservation, so too is the suicide rate devastating on the White Mountain Apache Reservation. In the United States, suicide was the third leading cause of death for youths ages 15–24, but for the White Mountain Apache Tribe, death rates for this age group were 13 times the U.S. average. In the United States, up to 500,000 persons a year required emergency care as a result of suicide attempts. At White Mountain, with only 15,500 tribal members, the Indian Service Hospital treated more than 200 youths a year for suicide attempts.[12]

The White Mountain Apaches were devastated by the problem but they tackled the problems of suicide with determination. They developed a suicide surveillance that required reporting to a centralized prevention task force, as well as training and employing a team of Apache case managers who followed up on every incident reported. The suicide prevention and intervention program worked with youth-at-risk, their families, and the elders, who impressed upon the youth that taking one's life was not the Apache way and taught them about the core strengths of their Apache heritage. This effort was the first community-based follow-up and triage system of its kind in the country.

In 2008, meth use in the state of Arizona was the biggest issue and the number one law enforcement problem. The White Mountain communities came together to form a coalition to carry out a campaign to develop awareness of meth and its devastating effects and adopt ordinances controlling over-the-counter cold medicines containing the drug needed to manufacture it.[13]

The High Rates of Obesity and Diabetes

Like the crime statistics in Indian country, the childhood obesity and diabetes rates in the last 30 years have also dramatically increased in Indian country, including among all the Apache tribes. Studies conducted during the 1990s revealed 39 percent of American Indian boys and 38 percent of American Indian girls were overweight, compared to 26 percent of white children.[14] Furthermore, studies found that 34 percent of American Indian women and 40 percent of American Indian men are obese.[15] While these figures are national averages, it can be safely assumed that they apply to the Apache people.

In general, the health and well-being of American Indian people since colonization has been poor. In the past several decades, behavioral and lifestyle factors have had great influence on the mortality rate in Indian communities. Currently, the leading causes of death among Indian adults include diabetes, heart disease, and cancer associated with obesity. The incidence of diabetes among Indians was 16.5 percent in 2005 and continues to increase. The hard fact is that obesity is a major health problem and is a great concern for Indian people, including the Apache people.

Many scholars agree that the increase in obesity and related chronic diseases can be attributed to the shift from active to sedentary lifestyles, the change from natural diets to those high in fat, and a general lack of physical activity. Other factors may include genetics and the environment. The pre-contact diet for the hunting and gathering Apache was based on wild game, like deer, elk, and buffalo, and edible plants, nuts, and berries. While the introduction of sheep and cattle replaced wild game, they were range fed and required a lot of physical exertion for their care and, therefore, did not radically change in the Apache diet.

It has been suggested that obesity became a serious health issue when the Apaches had a continuous and ample food supply that was neither nutritious nor genetically appropriate. Some scholars argue that the Apaches, as nomadic hunters, developed through evolution the ability for their bodies to use and store energy efficiently, permitting them to survive the feast-famine cycles. In other words, the feast-famine cycles controlled diabetes for individuals predisposed toward the disease because their metabolism enabled them to store fat during times of plenty and to efficiently use the stored energy during times of scarcity.[16]

As the Apaches were forcibly settled on reservations and thus unable to maintain hunter-gatherer activities over large territories, they became reliant on U.S. government–supplied foods, including flour, sugar, lard, beans, and canned meats. In the Indian boarding schools a wide array of white flour-based products like pasta, desserts, and dairy products were introduced to the Apache diet. A recent study has showed that wheat and dairy products are the main cause of diseases and obesity in O blood type people because their genetic makeup and evolution as hunter-gatherers does not support these types of foods. Native Americans are mainly O blood types.[17]

The food supply for Apaches increased with the establishment of grocery stores and restaurants both within and outside their reservations, so now the current diet includes processed foods that can be purchased at supermarkets and fast-food restaurants. One study indicated that beverages containing high-fructose corn syrup were a leading contributor to obesity among Native Americans.[18]

There are strong sentiments and preferences among many of the Apache people for foods that are frequently referred to as traditional foods or Indian foods. These traditional foods are items like the Apache tortilla and fry bread made of wheat flour mixed with baking powder and salt and deep fried in lard or oil. Some practices also include the liberal use of butter, lard, whole milk, fried meats and vegetables, as well as a generous use of fats in the preparation of beans, supplemented with sweets and snacks high in sugar. These so-called "traditional foods" are often more available than healthier alternatives and grace the dining tables of Apache families. If the family obtains commodity foods (foods distributed by the U.S. Department of Agriculture), they receive items like pastas, rice, white flour, and other foods high in fat and carbohydrates.[19]

Major factors affecting food choice on Apache reservations are the cost, availability, and shelf life. Many families have limited cash resources but purchase food on the reservation, where selection is limited and the cost is higher than in towns and cities that require travel to shop in. Furthermore, although housing conditions have improved for most Apache families, many tribal members do not live in homes with refrigerators, so fresh fruit and vegetables are infrequently on grocery shopping lists.[20]

Low socioeconomic status is one indicator for susceptibility to obesity and diabetes. People with lower incomes are more likely to have diets with a higher percentage of fat and lower percentages of food like fresh fruit and vegetables. It is a well-known statistic that more American Indians are economically disadvantaged compared with the general U.S. population. About 51 percent of American Indians residing on reservations live below the poverty level.[21]

PRESERVATION AND REVIVAL OF APACHE LANGUAGES

Revival of the Apache language and culture is a major concern for the Apache tribes. Despite the large number of native speakers among the Apaches, the younger generations are not learning how to speak the language. The language is not being passed down to the children. The decrease in the number of fluent language speakers has been attributed to social and economic factors both historically and in contemporary times, the effects of formal schooling for several generations, the advent of technology, changes in lifestyles and values, and outside influences.[22] There has also been the attitude, and often belief, of some of the Apaches that the language should not be passed on. For all these reasons, the revival, maintenance, and preservation of the Apache language have been formidable tasks and challenges.

For several decades, concerted efforts have been made by the Apache tribes to teach the Apache language, but most efforts have been less than successful. Although faced with overwhelming circumstances, the tribes have not given up. They see the survival of their religion, culture, and way of life tied to the revival of their language. An Apache leader stated that "our language is one of the most important connections we have to our history, our culture, our lands, and to our future as Apache people."[23] The tribal efforts have ranged from cooperative partnerships with professional linguists for the development of Apache dictionaries, textbooks, and curriculum materials, to sponsoring language immersion courses, and to having the Apache language taught in the public schools. The tribal collaborations with linguists to develop dictionaries have proved to be the most successful. The White Mountain, the San Carlos, and Jicarilla Apache tribes all have language dictionaries that were developed by a team of linguists and native speakers.[24]

The second effort that has been supported by the tribes has been the teaching of the language in the public schools on the reservations, from Head Start through high school. One Apache Head Start has been credited as a leader in the teaching of the Apache language within the mainstream school curriculum.[25] The classroom approach has been the most popular because of the amount of time students spend in school and because of the availability of teachers who already know "how to teach." While teaching the language in the public schools seemed like a natural solution, it has also been plagued with problems, like lack of adequate curriculum materials and shortage of teachers who are willing to teach the subject, the reluctant acceptance of the school system to teach the language, the lack of funding for "extracurricular" courses, and the lack of willingness by Apache students to take the courses when they are available.

Two issues that have contributed to why the teaching and learning of Apache has not been a raving success are the methods for teaching the language and the certification of the teachers. There has been a lack of adequate curriculum materials at various grade levels. The training of the teachers, both those with state-certified teaching certificates and Apache teachers who are either volunteers or paid, but with no state teaching credentials, has caused problems for the school systems. As a result of these types of problems, Apache language classes have not been offered consistently. The courses may be offered one year but not the next; the teacher may repeat materials covered the previous year because of lack of grade-level appropriate materials; the Apache teachers and volunteers do not have funding; or the school may decide not to offer the classes for one reason or another.

Adding to these classroom woes are the lack of tribal community and tribal leadership support, cooperation, and the "politicization" of the language programs by factions within the tribe who want to dominate the program, insist that the language should be taught only in a certain way, or will not cooperate because of the person who is teaching the classes. There is also a group that truly believes that the language should not be passed down to the next generations through the schools; that outsiders knowing the intricate details of the structure and meaning can only lead to further exploitation. There is also the belief that the linguists and researchers who study the Apache language are doing it only for reasons of their own, including mere curiosity and interest in enhancing their academic careers by publishing their studies; that despite their academic training and credentials, they really do not understand the Apache language because they superimpose the Western intellectual language acquisition models on a language that does not fit Western models or language paradigms.[26]

Knowing what efforts have been made in Indian country in the past has led to several new and important trends. These trends provide encouragement and shed light on the language revival and its future sustainability. Nationwide, Indian tribes have banded together to promote Congressional legislation to support language preservation efforts. The efforts began as early as 1974, when Congress authorized the passage of the Native American Programs Act. This act was reauthorized as the Esther Martinez Act of 2006. Through 2012, this act will provide a competitive grant program to promote, expand, replicate, or build on successful innovative language programs through projects like survival schools, teacher training, and immersion language restoration programs. National legislation has been supported by state and federal agencies, foundations and philanthropic organizations. Over the years, government agencies like the Administration for Native Americans (ANA) and the National and State Endowment for the Humanities have given grants to Indian tribes for language preservation projects. The National Science Foundation gave a grant to the Jicarilla Apache Tribe for developing its dictionary.

During Congressional hearings it was recognized that saving indigenous languages had wide support because it was understood that language is important in the way it shapes worldviews, values, and spiritual ceremonies. Halting the loss of Native languages was seen as linked to the building of self-confidence, promoting greater interest in school, creating intergenerational relationships, and encouraging language fluency and a way for fluent speakers to teach linguists. In short, "Indian tribes [were viewed as] living cultures that can contribute and be strengthened only through the perpetuation of their [language and] traditions."[27]

In addition to public support, language preservation, restoration, and maintenance have become important and critical issues among Native American scholars, linguists, communities, and individuals in general. In the last several decades they have been more proactive and active in expressing their views and in taking positive steps to be in the forefront of the language preservation movement. One such person is Bernadette Adley- SantaMaria, a doctoral candidate in linguistics at the University of Arizona and member and fluent speaker of the White Mountain Apache Tribe. While assisting at the University of Arizona's American Indian Language Development

Institute in developing a language textbook for the Western Apache, she had a hands-on opportunity not only to conduct a survey, but to evaluate the language revival program and offer recommendations from the perspective of a native speaker who understands her community and who has knowledge and direct experience with a tribal language program.

SantaMaria's views and recommendations were focused on the need for the involvement of committed and dedicated Native speakers in community-based language preservation programs, the need for tribal leadership support and advocacy, and for the tribes to participate and form partnerships with the academic community to continue their research and develop culturally sensitive and relevant language materials. She felt that schools could not be held responsible for reversing indigenous language loss and that the primary responsibility for language acquisition and preservation still rested with the family. Since the education of children was an all-encompassing process, learning the Apache language required the full support and effort of the individual, the family, the community, and the schools.

The collaboration between the academic community and native speakers was a critical element in the development of language textbooks. She was concerned about the way the language was taught using a Western model that concentrated on language structure, like verb paradigms that require taking verbs apart and analyzing the verb stems. This approach was making the learning of Apache unduly complicated, according to SantaMaria, because "Apache language verb stems by themselves make absolutely no sense." Fluent Apache speakers, even children, rarely make mistakes in grammar. In her opinion, "people almost never learn to speak a language fluently when writing and grammar were the focus but that just listening and talking, talking and listening was as important."[28]

Other Apache tribes have also recognized the critical need to involve native speakers in the language preservation efforts. The Jicarilla Apache Cultural Center conducted focus groups to determine what the programming priorities should be for the center as part of its overall planning.[29] It found that language preservation was the number one concern in the community. Among several approaches, it recognized that the native speakers had the major responsibility in language retention and its maintenance. In the past, the tribes' efforts had been focused on the teaching the spoken language in the schools, and the language preservation efforts were shouldered by a very small number of people in the schools and the community. The cultural center acknowledged that one additional tool in the arsenal of teaching and promotion of language acquisition was for native speakers to learn to read and write the language. In this way, native speakers could be certified as teachers, assist in developing curriculum materials, participate in the teaching of the language at home, and to begin to write down their stories in Apache. In short, the native speakers would take full responsibility for being the keepers of their language.

A Native American scholar summarized the role of Native Americans in reviving their languages. He argued that Indian people should not focus their energies on blaming the schools, the government, the churches, or the mass media for the damage they've done to the relationship between Indian people and their languages. Their energy and resources are better spent developing their own means to preserve their languages. He argues that the first and perhaps most critical step in this process is for Indian people to simply speak their languages at every opportunity.[30]

ENVIRONMENTAL PROTECTION BY THE APACHE TRIBES

The care and protection of the environment is on the top of the list of priorities for the Apache tribes, in the sense of bringing modern technology and scientific principles to their ancient worldview of living in harmony with nature. With just under 5 million acres (or 7,548 square miles) of reservation land collectively owned by the eight Apache tribes, it is almost a given that environmental protection is a natural and major concern for the tribes. In recent decades, the Apache tribes adopted sustained yield forest management for their 2 million acres of valuable timberlands in Arizona and New Mexico. On these lands, they have also subscribed to the scientific management of their fish and wildlife, created a diversified gene pool for their big game, and protected endangered species, like the Mexican spotted owl and gray wolf.

Natural resources have been the mainstay of their tribal economies, from the scenic lands and rivers which have been the foundation for tourism and outdoor recreation, to the abundance of grazing lands for the livestock. Throughout the United States, environmentalism has been a hot subject since the late 1960s, but for the Apache people, respecting nature in a reverential way has been a part of who they are as a people since time immemorial.

The White Mountain Apache Tribe's Wildlife and Outdoor Recreation Program manages all wildlife conservation and recreation activities. It operates its program as a self-sustaining tourism and recreation business enterprise in accordance with Apache values.[31] Up until the early 1980s, the tribe's game and fish department had little management control over its abundant natural and wildlife resources. The Arizona Game and Fish Department regulated, without tribal input, all non-member hunting activities and seasons, and set harvest levels on tribal lands. The state was issuing big game hunting permits at below market prices. White Mountain was witnessing the loss of a potential source of income.

The state control over tribal natural resources was a situation that the New Mexico Apache tribes were also faced with. Unable to allow state jurisdiction over their natural resources to continue, the Apache tribes supported each other and the issue eventually found its way to the U.S. Supreme Court in 1982 as *Mescalero Apache Tribe v. State of New Mexico*. This case recognized tribal sovereign authority over the management of tribal fish and wildlife resources and allowed the tribes full control over their natural resources. The White Mountain Apache Tribe developed a management system that included innovative and culturally appropriate businesses practices. Under tribal management, the big and small game hunting programs flourished. With the assistance of properly trained personnel and technicians like biologists, the tribe created "one of the most respected resource management programs in Indian Country" as well as the world. Its elk hunting program became a world-renowned trophy hunting program, along with hunts for pronghorn antelope, bighorn sheep, bear, and mountain lion. While preserving and creating a very healthy wildlife population and protecting endangered species, the tribe created a sustainable revenue stream using a balanced approach based on Apache values. Today the tribe receives about $600,000 annually in profits from its wildlife and recreation enterprises. In 2000, the Harvard Project on

Employees at the tribally owned and operated Alchesay Fish Hatchery on the White River Apache reservation in Arizona. (Copyright © Marilyn Angel Wynn/ Nativestock.com)

American Indian Economic Development honored this tribe with an award for its exemplary program, stating that the White Mountain Apache provided an example and important lesson for all Indian nations.

What gives this program an extra special dimension is how it understands that its effectiveness is directly tied to support from the community. Active involvement from elders is sought through an elders' advisory board. The advice of the elders led the tribe to broaden its list of sensitive species that went beyond that of the state or federal government. Understanding that, first and foremost, the bounty of the earth belonged to the people, a separate harvest system was established that included setting aside a separate hunting area on the reservation and designating special seasons for big game hunting. A conservation fund was set up to support hunter education, to report illegal poaching, and to provide college scholarships for tribal members. By reaching out to the tribal members and embracing their ideas, needs, and cultural connections to natural resources, the program was improved and its success was ensured. This program's achievements have become a tremendous source of pride for the White Mountain Apache Tribe. By combining prudent self-management, based on the needs and wants of the people, and excellence in enterprise management, based on state-of-the-art business practices, the White Mountain Apache Tribe has laid the foundation for a sustainable environment for generations to come.

THE JICARILLA APACHE TRIBE WILDLIFE FISHERIES PROGRAM

Joining its Apache brethren in Arizona, the Jicarilla Apache Tribe was a Harvard program honoree in 2000 for its environmental program involving the management of its elk and mule deer population, which is one of North America's largest.[32] The tribal Game and Fish Department operates and manages a 14,500-acre game park using state-of-the-art tracking systems and innovative environmental science technology to preserve the tribe's wildlife population. Its commitment is to protect the game and fish and its environment. In 1987 all mule deer hunting for a three-year period was suspended to allow population recovery of this species through measures including habitat improvement and predator control projects. It also eradicated a disease known as brucellosis from its captive elk herd. In 1993, the program successfully treated one of its largest lakes to prevent it from being taken over by carp and saving the trout.

The Jicarilla's Game and Fish Department has created the tribe's Game and Fish Code, one of the most comprehensive law enforcement codes regulating hunting and fishing in Indian country. The program has provided the tribe with a profitable annual income stream of about $500,000 that also helps fund other tribal programs. It has also catapulted the tribe's reputation for producing "more trophy mule deer than any other comparably sized area in North America."[33]

Significantly, the program has already begun to share its learning with Indian country and Canada's First Nations. It has held elk ranching seminars for tribal wildlife managers, and even the state of New Mexico has requested their assistance with the management of its mule deer population. Through long-term planning and commitment to scientific innovation, the Jicarilla Apaches' Game and Fish Department has become a model for government programs both within and outside Indian country.

SAN CARLOS APACHE TRIBE ELDERS PROGRAM

The role of elders in traditional Apache society was important in maintaining the families, governing the tribe, protecting the lands, practicing the religion, and teaching all the cultural ways. Cultural erosion has plagued modern Apache societies due to the changing times, technology, the federal government's economic and social policies, and the control of education by the dominant society. Consequently, the elders' position of respect and their role as advisors diminished dramatically in the twentieth century. Recognizing that this does not have to be the situation, in 1993, the San Carlos Apache Tribe recognized and revitalized the role of the elders by establishing the San Carlos Elders Cultural Advisory Council (ECAC) to advise the Tribal Council and the people of the tribe on all matters pertaining to cultural issues.[34] This Advisory Council plays a significant part in the governance of the tribe by advising on matters as diverse as natural resource management, environmental issues, leadership styles and responsibilities, and cultural practices. Anchored in the Apache belief that there is an innate and intimate spiritual connection between man and the natural world that requires respecting not only one's self but all other human beings and all living things, the elders rose to the challenge and took on their new responsibilities. The elders encouraged self-reliance and discouraged dependence on others. To them, being Apache means having the ability to think for one's self, knowing one's history, knowing how to speak the Apache language, participating in ceremonies, and acting responsibly and respectfully towards all living creatures.

The initial role of this Advisory Council was to classify, record, and identify the proper use of medicinal, food, and herbal plants; today it provides guidance on all environmental protection policies of the tribe's natural resources and its management. Notable policies that it advised on were the Mexican spotted owl surveys, reservation-based mining, and on how the federal and state agencies administer tribal lands, like the location of graves and sacred sites that should not be disturbed by the forestry department's tree harvesting programs. The ECAC made its views known when tribal members were being disrespectful and wasteful in the cutting and disposal of shade trees and scrub used for camps during the Sunrise Dances by publishing in the tribal newspaper the proper way to collect, use, and dispose of the materials. They also got the tribal council to be proactive in getting the U.S. Forest Service to change its policies when permit fees were required for tribal members to gather acorns in traditional hunting areas of the Tonto National Forest. The ECAC was instrumental in getting the U.S. Forest Service to provide special protection to two Apache sacred mountains, the San Francisco Peaks and Mount Graham.

The ECAC made one of its more significant contributions to tribal governance when it reminded the people about a time when leaders emerged because of their abilities, wisdom, and achievements and when important decisions were made in the best long-term interest of the nation. This reminder came in light of political upheaval, instability, financial mismanagement, and large tribal deficits. Committed to responsible tribal government, the ECAC gave voice to the traditional perspective on the proper management of both the people and the land.

The ECAC is a living testimonial to how elders can regain their traditional role as advisors and protectors of the social, economic, political, and spiritual well-being of an Indian tribe. The knowledge possessed by tribal elders is essential and invaluable to the health and general welfare of the Apache people, their environment, and tribal governance. The ECAC became an honoree of the Harvard Project on American Indian Economic Development in 2000 in recognition for serving as a conscience for the San Carlos Apache Tribe by honoring its own Apache values and for being "a keeper and carrier of traditional Apache wisdom [that] will benefit the tribe for generations to come."[35]

THE PROTECTION OF THE FEDERAL TRUST RELATIONSHIP

The federal trust responsibility for the general welfare of the Apache people, including their health, educational, and social welfare, remains a vital concern, and one that the Apache people will fight to maintain. The federal government's role as the trustee for the Apache tribes has been in existence since the mid-nineteenth century when the Apache tribes signed land cession treaties establishing peace between them and the people of the United States. As the U.S. military defeated peoples, Apaches agreed to confinement on Indian reservations in Arizona, New Mexico, and Oklahoma in exchange for giving up millions of acres of their homelands. The U.S. federal government agreed to provide protection of their lands and natural resources, and to provide for their general economic, social, and educational welfare. The tacit understanding was that the Apaches were to agree to become assimilated into the dominant society. The assimilation process was to be overseen by the federal government. The intent was for the Apache to give up their culture and language and religion. The federal government allowed and participated as an active agent to destroy the indigenous culture without regard to the damage to the Apache sense of self-worth as a tribe and as individuals. The consequences of this approach were long-term and deep-rooted.

The traditional Apache family structure has been eroding steadily over time and has been a major victim of assimilation efforts. Its marginalization and destruction has impacted a multitude of social, educational, and health-related issues. The consequences of the loss of culture have had a generational impact on crime, especially the use of meth, and on the health of the Apache people, especially diabetes and obesity. In dealing with these issues the tribes are attempting to revive the positive aspects of their culture, which includes the preservation of their languages and the protection of their environment.

Despite the problems that have been generated for the Apache people by the federal government, the trusteeship relationship between them is one that the Apache tribes will protect and maintain. The Apache tribes are determined that the people of the United States honor their historical agreements with the Apache people. The federal government has not only mismanaged its trust responsibilities but has created unnecessary barriers for the Apache people to be self-determined and self-sufficient. As the issues surrounding crime, the methamphetamine and its related issues, the rate of suicide, the critical health conditions, and the levels of poverty and unemployment rates continue to rise, the Apache tribes will need the assistance of their trustee as never before. Given adequate financial and technical assistance and the opportunity to take charge of their lives and destiny, the tribes have proven that they can make a difference for their people. The Apache people are motivated, have shown initiative, and have proven results. They have never been afraid to take on challenges, whether on the warpath defending their homelands or in protecting their environment using innovative technology. They realize that the ultimate responsibility for their welfare rests with themselves and are on the road to becoming truly self-determined.

Notes

1. U.S. Department of the Interior, Bureau of Indian Affairs, 25 CFR Part 70 RIN 1076-AD 98, "Certificate of Indian or Alaska Native Blood," in http://www.cita .chattanooga.org/bia/cdibfedreg.htm (accessed April 16, 2010).

2. Jack D. Forbes, "Blood Quantum: A Relic of Racism and Termination," from Native Intelligence, Column, November 27, 2000 in "the People's Paths!" NAIIP News Path!, http://www.yvwiiusdinvnohii.net/Articles2000/JDForbes001126 Blood.htm (accessed April 16, 2010).

3. Ibid.

4. National Congress of American Indians (NCAI), "Methamphetamines in Indian Country: An American Problem Uniquely Affecting Indian Country," November 2006. (Hereinafter cited as NCAI Meth in Indian Country.) Footnote 4, 2.

5. Ibid.

6. Ibid., 1.

7. Ibid., 2.

8. "Testimony of Chairwoman Kathleen W. Kitcheyan of the San Carlos Apache Tribe for the Oversight Hearing on The Problem of Methamphetamine in Indian Country Before the Committee on Indian Affairs, U.S. Senate," April 5, 2006, 2. http://indian.senate.gov/public/_files/Kitcheyan040506.pdf (hereinafter cited as San Carlos Testimony).

9. Roe Bubar & Diane Payne, "Methamphetamine and Child Abuse in Native America," in http://www.ncai.org/ncai/Meth/Methamphetamine_and_Child_Abuse _in_Native_America_Article.pdf 1.

10. San Carlos Testimony, 2.

11. San Carlos Testimony, 4–8.

12. Testimony of Novalene Goklish, Senior Program Coordinator, White Mountain Apache Youth Suicide Prevention Program, from: http://indian.senate.gov/public/_files/NovaleneGoklishtestimony.pdf (accessed April 15, 2010).

13. Mara Reyes, "Terry Goddard Praises White Mountain Communities' approach to meth problem," The White Mountain Independent's online edition, August 15, 2008, http:///www.wmicentral.com (accessed April 15, 2010).

14. "War on Obesity Vital for Youngsters," *Indian Country Today*, Editorials, from http://www.indiancountrytoday.com/opinion/editorials/84224587.html (accessed on February 22, 2010.

15. Mary Story, et al., "The epidemic of obesity in American Indian communities and the need for childhood obesity-prevention programs," *American Journal of Clinical Nutrition* Vol. 69, No. 4, 747S-754S, April 1999 from http://www.ajcn.org/content/full/69/4/747S#FN1 (accessed April 16, 2010), (hereinafter cited as Story, *Epidemic of Obesity*).

16. Ibid., 5.

17. Peter J. D'Adamo, *The GenoType Diet: Change Your Genetic Destiny* (New York: Broadway Books, 2007) 3–14.

18. "Beverage Consumption and Risk of Obesity among Native Americans in Arizona," *Nutrition Reviews*, Vol. 62, Issue 4, June 28, 2008 from http://www3 .interscience.wiley.com/journal/119821977/abstract?CRETRY=1&SRETRY=0, 1 (accessed April 16, 2010).

19. Sharma, Sangita, Xia Cao, Joel Gittelsohn, Becky Ethelbah, and Jean Anliker, "Nutritional Composition of Commonly Consumed Traditional Apache Foods in Arizona," *International Journal of Food Sciences and Nutrition*, February, 2008; 59(1): 1-10.

20. Story, *Epidemic of Obesity*, 6.

21. Ibid.

22. Bernadette Adley-SantaMaria, "White Mountain Apache Language: Issues in Language Shift, Textbook Development, and Native Speaker-University Collaboration,"

Chapter 12, Teaching Indigenous Languages, (Northern Arizona University, 1997) from http://jan.ucc.nau.edu/~jar/TIL_12.html (accessed May 10, 2010) (hereinafter cited as SantaMaria, White Mountain Apache Language).

23. David Reede, Vice Chairman, San Carlos Apache Tribe, Issues/Initiatives, Culture and Language Preservation, from http://www.scatvicechairmanreede.com/ issues/initiatives.html (accessed May 11, 2010).

24. For examples of Apache dictionaries, see Willem Joseph de Reuse and Phillip Goode, *A Practical Grammar of the San Carlos Apache Language*, Volume 51 of LIN-COM studies in Native American linguistics; Dorothy Bray, ed., *Western Apache-English Dictionary: A Community-Generated Bilingual Dictionary*; Wilma Phone and Maureen Olsen, Matilda Martinez, *Dictionary of Jicarilla Apache*, Albuquerque: University of New Mexico Press, 2007.

25. "Apache Education," American Public University, from http://www.members .Tripod.com/archaeology_man/education.html (accessed May 10, 2010).

26. SantaMaria, "White Mountain Apache Language."

27. "Native Language Given a Boost," Friends Committee on National Legislation, March 14, 2008, from http://www.fcnl.org/issues/item.php?item_id=2217&issue_id =96 (accessed May 11, 2010).

28. SantaMaria, "White Mountain Apache Language."

29. "Language Is Number One Priority" press release, April, etc.

30. R. Littlebear, "Teaching American Indian and Alaska Native Languages in the Schools: What Has Been Learned. ERIC Digest," ERIC Clearinghouse on Rural Education and Small Schools, from http://www.ericdigests.org/2000-4/native.htm (accessed May 11, 2010).

31. The Harvard Project on American Indian Economic Development, John F. Kennedy School of Government, Harvard University, "Wildlife and Outdoor Recreation Program, White Mountain Apache Tribe (Whiteriver, AZ)," Honoring Nations Honoree 2000, in Veronica E. Tiller, compiler, *Tiller's Guide to Indian Country: Economic Profiles of American Indian Reservations* (Albuquerque: BowArrow Publishing Co., 2005), 301–302.

32. The Harvard Project on American Indian Economic Development, John F. Kennedy School of Government, Harvard University, "Wildlife and Fisheries Management Program, Game and Fish Department, Jicarilla Apache Tribe," Honoring Nations Honoree 1999, in Veronica E. Tiller, compiler, *Tiller's Guide to Indian Country: Economic Profiles of American Indian Reservations* (Albuquerque: BowArrow Publishing Co., 2005), 733.

33. Ibid.

34. The Harvard Project on American Indian Economic Development, John F. Kennedy School of Government, Harvard University, "Elders Cultural Advisory Council Forest Resources," Honoring Nations Honoree 2000, in Veronica E. Tiller, compiler, *Tiller's Guide to Indian Country: Economic Profiles of American Indian Reservations* (Albuquerque: BowArrow Publishing Co., 2005), 350–351.

35. Ibid.

Selected Bibliography

Books

Ball, Eve, Nora Henn, and Lynda Sanchez. *Indeh: An Apache Odyssey*. Provo: Brigham Young University Press, 1982.

Beck, Peggy, Anna Lee Walters, and Nia Francisco. *The Sacred: Ways of Knowledge, Sources of Life*. Tsaile: Navajo Community College Press, 1996.

Boyer, Ruth McDonald, and Narcissus Duffy Gayton. *Apache Mothers and Daughters: Four Generations of a Family*. Norman: University of Oklahoma Press, 1992.

Bray, Dorothy, ed., *Western Apache–English Dictionary: A Community-Generated Bilingual Dictionary*. Tempe: Bilingual Press/Editorial Bilingue, 1998.

Clark, LaVerne Harrell. *They Sang for Horses: The Impact of the Horse on Navajo & Apache Folklore*. Boulder: University of Colorado Press, 1966.

Cremony, John C. *Life Among the Apaches*. San Francisco: A. Roman & Company, 1868.

Davis, Mary B., Editor, *Native America in the Twentieth Century: An Encyclopedia*, New York: Garland Publishing Inc., 1994.

Davis, Michael G. *Ecology, Sociopolitical Organization, and Cultural Change on the Southern Plains, A Critical Treatise in the Sociocultural Anthropology of Native North America*. Kirksville, Missouri: Thomas Jefferson University Press, 1996.

Debo, Angie. *Geronimo: The Man, His Time, His Place*. Norman: University of Oklahoma Press, 1976.

De Reuse, Willem Joseph, and Phillip Goode. "A Practical Grammar of the San Carlos Apache Language." Volume 51 of LINCOM studies in Native American linguistics. Muenchen: LINCOM Europe, 2006.

Farrer, Claire R. *Living Life's Circle: Mescalero Apache Cosmovision*. Albuquerque: University of New Mexico Press, 1991.

Gibson, Arrell Morgan. *The American Indian: Prehistory to the Present*. Lexington, MA: D. C. Heath & Company, 1980.

Gomez, Arthur R., and Veronica E. Tiller. *Fort Apache Forestry: A History of Timber Management and Forest Protection on the Fort Apache Indian Reservation, 1870–1985*. Albuquerque: Tiller Research, Inc., 1990.

Harvard Project on American Indian Economic Development. *The State of the Native Nations*. New York & Oxford: Oxford University Press, 2008.

Hirschfelder, Arlene, and Martha Kreipe de Montaño. *The Native American Almanac: A Portrait of Native America Today*. New York: Prentice Hall General Reference, 1993.

Historical Research Associates. *The Mescalero Timber Trust: A History of Forest Management on the Mescalero Indian Reservation, New Mexico*. Missoula: Mountain Moving Press, 1981.

Jicarilla Apache Community Education Video Program. *Jicarilla Apache Pottery*. Dulce: Jicarilla Apache Tribe, 1982.

Kelly, Lawrence C. *The Assault on Assimilation: John Collier and the Origins of Indian Policy Reform*. Albuquerque: University of New Mexico Press, 1983.

Lieder, Michael, and Jake Page. *Wild Justice: The People of Geronimo vs. the United States*. New York: Random House, 1997.

Mails, Thomas. *The People Called Apache*. Englewood Cliffs, New Jersey: Prentice Hall, Inc., 1974.

Nordhaus, Robert J. *Tipi Rings: A Chronicle of the Jicarilla Apache Land Claim*. Albuquerque: BowArrow Publishing Company, 1995.

O'Brien, Sharon. *American Indian Tribal Governments*. Norman: University of Oklahoma Press, 1989.

O'Donnell, Joan K., ed. *Here, Now, and Always: Voices of the First Peoples of the Southwest*. Santa Fe: Museum of New Mexico Press, 2001.

Perlman, Barbara H. *Allan Houser (Ha-o-zous)*. Santa Fe: Glenn Green Galleries, 1992 Edition.

Pesata, Lydia, et al. *Jicarilla Basket Making*. A Project of Native Arts and Crafts Cultural Awareness Program, ESAA. Loveland, Colorado: Center for In-Service Education, 1975.

Phone, Wilhelmina, Maureen Olson, and Matilda Martinez. *Dictionary of Jicarilla Apache*. Albuquerque: University of New Mexico Press, 2007.

Rushing III, W. Jackson. *Allan Houser, An American Master (Chiricahua Apache, 1914–1994)*. New York: Harry N. Abrams, Inc., Publishers, 2004.

Semos Unlimited. *Nuevo Mexico: An Anthology of History*. Las Vegas: New Mexico Highlands University, 2009.

Sonnichsen, C. L. *The Mescalero Apaches*. Norman: University of Oklahoma Press, 1973, second ed.

Stockel, H. Henrietta. *Chiricahua Apache Women and Children: Safekeepers of the Heritage*. Texas A&M University Press, 2000.

Stockel, H. Henrietta. *Women of the Apache Nation: Voices of Truth*. Reno: University of Nevada, 1991.

Tanner, Clara Lee. *Apache Indian Baskets*. Tucson: University of Arizona Press, 1982.

Thrapp, Dan L. *The Conquest of Apacheria*. Norman: University of Oklahoma Press, 1967.

Thrapp, Dan L. *Victorio and the Mimbres Apaches*. Norman: University of Oklahoma Press, 1974.

Tiller, Veronica. *The Jicarilla Apache Tribe: A History*. Albuquerque: BowArrow Publishing, 1983.

Tiller, Veronica, comp. *Tiller's Guide to Indian Country: Economic Profiles of American Indian Reservations*, Albuquerque: BowArrow Publishing Co., 2005.

Utley, Robert M. *Frontier Regulars: The United States Army and the Indian, 1866–1891*, Bloomington: Indiana University Press, 1973.

Warren, Nancy Hunter. *The Jicarilla Apache: A Portrait*. Albuquerque: University of New Mexico Press, 2006.

Weigle, Marta, Frances Levine, and Louise Stiver. *Telling New Mexico: A New History*. Santa Fe: Museum of New Mexico Press, 2009.

Whiteford, Andrew Hunter. *Southwestern Indian Baskets: Their History and Their Makers*. Santa Fe: School of American Research Press, 1989.

Williamson, Ray A. *Living the Sky: The Cosmos of the American Indian*. Norman: University of Oklahoma Press, 1987.

Worcester, Donald E. *The Apaches: Eagles of the Southwest*. Norman: University of Oklahoma Press, 1979.

Articles

Bahr, K. S. "The Strengths of Apache Grandmothers: Observations on Commitment, Culture, and Caretaking." *Journal of Comparative Family Studies* 25(2): 233–248.

Basso, Keith. "Western Apache." In *Handbook of North American Indians*, vol. 10: *Southwest*, edited by Alfonso Ortiz. Washington, D.C.: Smithsonian Institution Press, 1983.

Jackson, Devon. "The Big Picture." *Santa Fean*, August 2002, 48–55.

Nicholas, Dan. "Mescalero Apache Girls' Puberty Feast." *El Palacio* XLVI (September, 1939): 9.

Opler, Morris E. "Chiricahua Apache." In *Handbook of North American Indians*, vol. 10: *Southwest*, edited by Alfonso Ortiz. Washington, D.C.: Smithsonian Institution Press, 1983.

Opler, Morris E. "The Mescalero Apache." In *Handbook of North American Indians*, vol. 10: *Southwest*, edited by Alfonso Ortiz. Washington, D.C.: Smithsonian Institution Press, 1983.

Sharma, Sangita, Xia Cao, Joel Gittelsohn, Becky Ethelbah, and Jean Anliker. "Nutritional Composition of Commonly Consumed Traditional Apache Foods in Arizona." *International Journal of Food Sciences and Nutrition* 59(1): 1–10.

Tiller, Veronica E. "The Jicarilla Apache." In *Handbook of North American Indians*, vol. 10: *Southwest*, edited by Alfonso Ortiz. Washington, D.C.: Smithsonian Institution Press, 1983.

Tiller, Veronica E. "Westward Expansion, Indian Wars, and Reservations (1850–1900)." In *Encyclopedia of American Indian History*, Vol. I, edited by Bruce E. Johansen and Barry M. Pritzker. Santa Barbara: ABC-CLIO, 2008:39–49.

Turcheneske Jr., John Anthony. "The United States Congress and the Release of the Apache Prisoners of War at Fort Sill." *Chronicles of Oklahoma* 54:1 (1976): 200–226.

Robert W. Young. "Apachean Languages." In *Handbook of North American Indians*, vol. 10: *Southwest*, edited by Alfonso Ortiz. Washington, D.C.: Smithsonian Institution Press, 1983.

Studies and Ph.D. Dissertations

Ball, Martin W. "Mountain Spirits: Embodying the Sacred in Mescalero Apache Tradition." Ph.D. diss., University of California, Santa Barbara, 2000. UMI Dissertation Services, Ann Arbor, Michigan.

Hall, Jan Erik. "Apache Cattle: The Reservation as Marketplace, a Sale Yard Feasibility Study." Harvard Project on American Indian Economic Development, John F. Kennedy School of Government, Harvard University, PRS 88-11, May 1988.

National Congress of American Indians (NCAI). "Methamphetamines in Indian Country: An American Problem Uniquely Affecting Indian Country." November 2006.

Government Sources

U.S. Census Bureau, *We the People: American Indians and Alaska Natives in the United States*, Census 2000 Special Reports, (U.S. Department of Commerce, February 2006).

U.S. Census Bureau, 2004 American Community Survey, Selected Population Profiles, "Table 2. American Indian and Alaska Native Household Population by Tribal Group: 2004, *The American Community—American Indians and Alaska Natives: 2004*."

U.S. Census Bureau, "Figure 1. Selected Age Groups and Median Age: 2000," *We the People: American Indians and Alaska Natives in the United States*, Census 2000 Special Reports, (U. S. Department of Commerce, February 2006).

U.S. Census Bureau, 2004 American Community Survey, Selected Population Profiles, "Figure 2. Responsibility for Grandchildren Under 18 Years: 2004, *The American Community—American Indians and Alaska Natives: 2004*."

U.S. Census Bureau, 2004 American Community Survey, Selected Population Profiles, "Figure 4. Marital Status: 2004, *The American Community—American Indians and Alaska Natives: 2004*."

Web Sites

Adley-SantaMaria, Bernadette. "White Mountain Apache Language: Issues in Language Shift, Textbook Development, and Native Speaker-University Collaboration," Chapter 12 in *Teaching Indigenous Languages*. Northern Arizona University, 1997. http://jan.ucc.nau.edu/~jar/TIL_12.html (accessed May 10, 2010).

Bubar, Roe, and Diane Payne. "Methamphetamine and Child Abuse in Native America." http://www.ncai.org/ncai/Meth/Methamphetamine_and_Child_Abuse_in_Native_America_Article.pdf, 1.

Forbes, Jack D. "Blood Quantum: A Relic of Racism and Termination." Native Intelligence, Column, November 27, 2000, in "the People's Paths!" NAIIP News Path! http://www.yvwiiusdinvnohii.net/Articles2000/JDForbes001126 Blood.htm (accessed April 16, 2010).

Indian Country Today. "War on Obesity Vital for Youngsters." http://www.indian countrytoday.com/opinion/editorials/84224587.html (accessed February 22, 2010).

Story, Mary, et al. "The Epidemic of Obesity in American Indian Communities and the Need for Childhood Obesity-Prevention Programs." *American Journal of Clinical Nutrition* 69: 4, 747S–754S, April 1999. http://www.ajcn.org/content/full/69/4/747S#FN1 (accessed April 16, 2010).

U.S. Census, American Indian Statistics by Social and Economic Factors 2000 Census, "Percentage of non-English Language Use in AIAN Areas Persons 5 and older." http://www.ovc.edu/missions/indians/indsocia.htm (accessed March 30, 2010).

Government Sources from Web Sites

National American Indian Housing Council. "Indian Housing Fact Sheet." http://www.naihc.net/news/index.asp?bid=6316 (accessed March 29, 2010).

"Testimony of Chairwoman Kathleen W. Kitcheyan of the San Carlos Apache Tribe for the Oversight Hearing on the Problem of Methamphetamine in Indian Country Before the Committee on Indian Affairs, U.S. Senate." April 5, 2006. http://indian.senate.gov/public/_files/Kitcheyan040506.pdf

"Testimony of Novalene Goklish, Senior Program Coordinator, White Mountain Apache Youth Suicide Prevention Program." http://indian.senate.gov/public/_files/NovaleneGoklishtestimony.pdf (accessed April 15, 2010).

U.S. Bureau of the Census. "Statistical Brief, Housing of American Indians on Reservations – Structural Characteristics, 1990." http://www.ewebtribe.com/NACulture/articles/IndianHousingStats.htm (accessed March 30, 2010).

U.S. Census Bureau, American FactFinder. "New Mexico–American Indian Area, GCT-PH1. Population, Housing Units, Area, and Density: 2000." http://www.factfinder.census.gov (accessed March 23, 2010).

U.S. Census Bureau, American FactFinder. "Profile of General Demographic Characteristics: 2000, Data Set: Census 2000 American Indian and Alaska

Native Summary Files, Apache Alone, (A-09-A-23) Apache alone (A09-A-23) or in any combination." http://www.factfinder.census.gov (accessed April 1, 2010).

U.S. Census Bureau, American FactFinder. Quick Tables, "DP – 1. Profile of General Demographic Characteristics: 2000, Apache Alone (A09-A-23)." http://www.factfinder.census.gov (accessed April 1, 2010).

U.S. Indian Health Service. "Facts on Indian Health Disparities, January 2006." http://info.ihs.gov/Files/DisparitiesFacts-Jan2006.pdf (accessed March 30, 2010).

Index

Page numbers in italics refer to photographs.

About the Author

VERONICA E. VELARDE TILLER is a Jicarilla Apache writer of Native American history, and editor and publisher of the award-winning economic reference guide covering 562 modern Indian tribes: *Tiller's Guide to Indian Country*. She is CEO for Tiller Research, Inc., in Albuquerque, New Mexico.